THE
ABORTION
PAPERS
IRELAND

Edited by

Ailbhe Smyth

Attic Press
Dublin

First published in Ireland 1992 by
Attic Press
4 Upper Mount Street
Dublin 2

British Library Cataloguing in Publication Data
Abortion Papers, Ireland
    I. Smyth, Ailbhe
    363.4

    ISBN 1 855940 450

Cover Design: Attic Press
Origination: Attic Press
Printing: Colour Books Ltd, Dublin

Acknowledgements
The editor and publisher are grateful to Irish Women's Abortion
Support Group for their permission to include 'Across the Water', which
first appeared in *Feminist Review* No.29, Spring 1988; to Pauline Conroy
Jackson and Galway University Press for permission to reproduce
'Outside the Jurisdiction: Irish Women Seeking Abortion', from C
Curtin, P Jackson, B O'Connor (Eds) (1987): *Gender in Irish Society*; to
NIALRA for permission to reproduce an extract from *Why We Need the
1967 Abortion Act* (NIALRA, 1985); to Jo Murphy-Lawless and Ablex
Publishing for permission to reproduce 'The Obstetric View of Feminine
Identity' from A D Dodd and S Fisher (Eds) (1988); *Gender and Discourse:
The Power of Talk*; 'The Death of Ann Lovett' was included in Nell
McCafferty; *The Best of Nell* (Attic Press, 1984); 'As Far as Practicable ...'
was included in Nell McCafferty; *Goodnight Sisters* (Attic Press, 1987);
'Towards a Feminist Morality of Choice' is extracted from Ruth Riddick;
The Right to Choose - Questions of Feminist Morality (Attic Press, 1990).

Contents

Preface

Abortion has been a fact of Irish women's lives for centuries, just as it has been and continues to be for women elsewhere. In Ireland, however, control of women's reproduction has been exercised with particular severity since the nineteenth century. The legal availability of contraception, for example, which was a major issue for the women's movement in Ireland throughout the 1970s, has remained a matter of political debate right up to the present, and is still far from being satisfactorily resolved. In 1983, despite the existence of legislation definitively prohibiting abortion, the Constitution was amended by referendum to include a clause guaranteeing both the 'right to life of the unborn' and 'the right to life of the mother'.

Over the past three decades, profound economic and social changes, including the impact of feminist resistance and questioning of women's status and roles, have begun to erode traditional ideologies and practices. Value systems and mechanisms of social and moral control, strongly marked by a deeply catholic ethos, have been seriously challenged in a variety of ways, some direct and explicit, others as a consequence of the process of change itself. In effect, the traditional bases of Irish society have been destabilised, most noticeably where the control of women's sexuality and reproductive functions is concerned.

It is something of a cliché to point to the 'crisis' in the Irish state. Nonetheless, the lengths to which the most conservative elements in Irish society are prepared to go to impose their position on the population as a whole, and the ferocity with which they defend their ideology indicate a sense of disarray and a deep fear of change. The clash between traditional ideologies and value systems and progressive forces of change has been a very real one in Ireland over the past decade. It has erupted, and been

4

barely contained, on several occasions but eventually reached a crisis point in the events of early spring 1992, when a fourteen-year old rape victim was prevented by the High Court from travelling abroad to seek a safe, legal abortion. The Supreme Court overruled the High Court decision and, in its ruling, declared that abortion may be deemed legal in Ireland in certain limited circumstances.

This pivotal case, and the dramatic Supreme Court judgement, gave rise to the most intensely divisive debate on abortion in Ireland since 1983. The debate absorbed the attention of the entire country for several months, a sign of the extent to which people generally, if sometimes obscurely, perceive abortion as a crucially important defining issue for the society and culture as a whole.

This collection of essays arose from the need to create a space where both the historical and contemporary complexity of abortion as a social, political and ethical issue of paramount importance to women, could be discussed within a feminist framework. A considered, reflective exploration of the politics and the morality of abortion has been unusually difficult to achieve in the pressured and emotive atmosphere which has surrounded the issue. Irish feminist scholars and activists (and often the two are one and the same) have indeed initiated such discussions and have written significantly on abortion from a number of different perspectives. Given the centrality of abortion in terms of our lives as women and its definitional importance for Ireland as a modern European state, it seemed to be an urgent necessity to bring together some of the most important feminist thinking on the issue and thus, I hope, contribute to a more informed and acute analysis, one which takes fully into account the realities and the needs of women.

Obviously, this book would not have been possible without the authors, all of whom responded so positively to my outline of the project. They undertook to write or revise their contributions in a remarkably short time-span and I am immensely grateful to them. I would also like to thank those authors and publishers who kindly and speedily gave permission to reprint essays and articles. A special 'thank you' to Therese Caherty for her prompt help. As always, my warmest thanks to everyone in Attic Press for their commitment, support and hard work in bringing this book to press: Sinéad Bevan, Marie Cotter, Gráinne Healy, Maeve Kneafsey and Orla Pearse, and also to Eleanor Ashe for her careful work on the manuscript. To Róisín Conroy I owe a great deal, for which my gratitude.

This book is dedicated to all Irish women who have ever had to travel abroad for an abortion.

Ailbhe Smyth
Summer 1992

A Sadistic Farce
Women and Abortion in the Republic of Ireland, 1992

Prologue: About Meaning, Language and Value

In February 1992, a fourteen-year-old Irish rape victim was prevented by a High Court injunction from leaving the jurisdiction of Ireland to obtain an abortion in Britain. Early in March, following an appeal to the Supreme Court lodged by her family on her behalf, the girl was permitted to leave the jurisdiction. It is understood that she then went to Britain where her pregnancy was terminated.

Put as baldly as this, what has come to be known as the X case seems straightforward, although shocking. In point of fact, it is an extremely complicated case with the most serious consequences for the reproductive freedoms of Irish women and disturbing implications for their rights as citizens of Ireland and of Europe. The case derives directly from the anti-abortion amendment to the Constitution (the Eighth Amendment), inserted by a bitterly divisive referendum in 1983. Further, the case rapidly became entangled with Ireland's imminent ratification of the Maastricht Treaty on European Union. As I write, in June 1992, the levels of political confusion, legal ambiguity and profound personal distress which have been compounded since February continue to reverberate throughout the Irish social and political system, with every indication that the situation will become even more intricate and divisive over the coming months.

Even within Ireland, it has been exceptionally difficult to make sense of a situation which has consistently been framed in highly technical legal language, and further obscured by layers of 'Euro-speak' and political whitewash. For much of the time over the past several months, it has seemed as though we are living in a nightmare version of Alice's Wonderland where words can mean whatever lawyers and politicians want them to mean - without any reference to the material realities they supposedly signify. Women's bodies, women's right to bodily integrity, women's freedom to control our reproductive processes are caught in an impenetrable, materially meaningless web of male-generated words.

For of course, women have been signally absent from a debate which concerns them in the most immediate, intimate and serious ways possible. Just two weeks after the case of the fourteen-year-old girl came to light, the Dáil (*Irish Parliament*) belatedly decided to allot limited time to a discussion of the issue. During the course of the debate, Deputy Monica Barnes requested 'one minute of the House's time on behalf of the women of Ireland', only to be ruled out of order by the Chair and invited to show 'respect' for the rules of the House. A woman journalist present in the House commented as follows:

If ever there was a metaphor for a society in which men control the structures of power and are determined to keep it that way, it was the Dáil yesterday afternoon. There were nine women deputies in the chamber and row upon row of middle-aged men in suits.[1] [....] This week, at least 100 women will travel to England for abortions. It will be an even more desolate journey than usual because of what has happened in recent days. It is shameful, but not alas, surprising that no woman was allowed to speak for them in what a former Taoiseach (Prime Minister) once described as the 'democratic forum of the nation'. (Mary Holland, *The Irish Times* 19/02/92)

What women are experiencing in Ireland at present is the literal and literally frightening power of language to constitute social reality. Language is used, in quite explicit and transparent ways, to construct or to deny the contours and material substance of women's lives. Control through discourse is almost naïvely exposed in the present Irish controversy. Women's sexuality and reproduction are confined by politico-legal linguistic formulae (ie, by being referred to in restrictive or reductive ways in Constitutional amendments, protocols and solemn declarations), or paradoxically defined as non-existent (ie, by not being spoken at all).[2]

Discussing the implications for women of the X case and of the Maastricht Treaty, Frances Fitzgerald, Chairwoman of the Irish Council for the Status of Women[3], described the process whereby Irish women have been

8

reduced by words to a half-life, or have disappeared out of life altogether:

Of course words are important: it is words in 1983, and more recently in relation to Maastricht, which have brought us to this situation [...] It is interesting to me that so many men have been so prominent on this issue both now and when I reflect on 1983. On the one hand, it points to the fact that it is men who make decisions in Irish life, but on the other hand it points out how little comment so many of these very same men make on other women's issues. (Frances Fitzgerald)[4]

The language of the self-styled 'Pro-Life' movement consciously plays with ethical and biological meanings of 'life' (Pre-life/Pro-Life), re-investing 'Life' with a new (capitalised) foetocentric meaning. Words conjure up a new hierarchy of 'life' values in which the foetus is promoted to the status of 'baby', while women are 'demoted' to the materially undervalued condition of 'mother'. In Pro-Life discourse, women lose their independent lives and are deprived of their civil status: women are represented consistently and exclusively as 'mothers'. As the foetus plays an increasingly visible role in Pro-Life discourse, women become decreasingly visible: for women, the 'law' is one of diminishing returns.

A woman letter-writer to *The Irish Times* identified both the absurdity and the danger of this word 'play' perfectly: since, she mused, the 'unborn' have special Constitutional protections (including exemption from payment of taxes), could these protections not also be extended to the 'undead' (including non-payment of taxes)? But it is one thing to play with words, and quite another to play with lives. Or is it? In nuclear physics, the half-life of a substance is the length of time it takes for a unit of that substance to reduce to half of its original value.[5] How long would it take to reduce women to no value at all?

If it has been difficult for Irish people to understand the constantly changing complexities of the current situation, I suspect it appears utterly incomprehensible to everyone else. Were it not for the indisputable fact that the 'real life' value of women is at stake, it must surely seem like a farce. Which perhaps it is: a sadistic farce dreamed up by a viciously controlling consortium of right-wing conspirators. What is the current value on the export market of a pregnant Irish woman? This is no joke in Ireland in 1992. It is a deadly serious reality.

But while the farce-makers act out their sadistic joke on the public stage, women in Ireland considering or seeking abortions abroad continue to do so in private anguish, uncertain about the legal status of their actions and without the information and practical support which would help to make their journey less traumatic.

Act 1: The X Case

The details of the case which provoked unprecedented outrage and confusion in Ireland, and which exposed the extent and strength of patriarchal control of women's bodies, are complicated and technical. In recalling them, I was struck by how closely women's reproductive functions are 'policed' by legal discourse, struck too by how totally women's physical, mental and social experiences are evacuated by that discourse.

On 6 February 1992, the Attorney General (principal law officer of the state) obtained an interim injunction restraining a pregnant fourteen-year-old girl who had been raped from seeking an abortion in the UK[6]. The Attorney General cited as the basis for his action Article 40.3.3 of the Constitution, the notorious Eighth Amendment of 1983. The relevant clause reads:

The state acknowledges the right to life of the unborn and, with due regard to the right to life of the mother, guarantees in its laws to respect, and, as far as practicable, by its laws to defend and vindicate that right.

Briefly, the Attorney General's justification for his action was that he had clear evidence that a foetus with guaranteed rights under the Constitution was about to be aborted and that he must act immediately to prevent this in his capacity as protector of the people's Constitutional rights.

The evidence had come to the Attorney General's attention through the Irish police. The girl and her parents had actually gone to the UK so that the pregnancy could be terminated, but before the abortion was carried out they had contacted the Irish police to check whether a DNA test would be admissible as forensic evidence in seeking to prove paternity. Following the interim injunction, the girl and her parents returned to Ireland, no doubt concerned by the possible legal consequences of simply ignoring it. Such is the mystifyingly intimidatory force of the law.

The injunction was confirmed by the High Court on 17 February and the girl and her parents were prohibited from leaving Ireland 'for a period of nine months from the date hereof'. As Emily O'Reilly comments: 'The state in effect was forcing the girl to have the rapist's child with the threat of possible imprisonment hanging over her head if she failed to comply.'[7] The power of the state to confine women within its jurisdiction and to deprive them of the right to freedom of movement could not have been made more explicit. Strictly speaking, the logical but effectively unworkable consequence of the High Court injunction was that all pregnant women in Ireland (of whatever nationality) could henceforth be interned within a 'police state' on the basis that they could or might seek an abortion when they went abroad. As a sister academic and social policy analyst put it so vividly, and accurately: 'The state is convulsed, with us inside it'.[8]

In his ruling, the High Court judge, Declan Costello, had argued that although X had specifically told both her parents and the police that she felt suicidal ('I feel like throwing myself down the stairs' and 'I feel like throwing myself under a train'), the risk to her life was not equal to the 'real and imminent danger to the life of the unborn'. This fourteen-year-old girl's life was callously calculated by the judge as less valuable than that of the foetus she was carrying - a foetus, furthermore, biologically dependent for its 'life' on her continuing to live. The foetus was entitled, according to the judge's logic, to the absolute protection of the law, while the threat of suicide on the part of the fourteen-year-old pregnant girl could be averted by the love and care of her family 'during the difficult months ahead'.

The simultaneously tragic and ludicrous irony of the

judgement was that legally X was a minor, a child. In Ireland, therefore, and according to the law, the 'right-to-life' of the unborn took precedence over the right to *live* of born children.

Justice Costello also argued, among other points, that Ireland was free to do as it pleased in relation to abortion law, even when it had extra-territorial implications, as abortion constituted public policy and was therefore immune to EC challenge.[9] Ireland was, despite the imminence of European Union, a 'law unto itself'. It must be said that Justice Costello spoke the strict truth, for where abortion legislation is concerned Ireland is indeed unique among the twelve member states of the EC.

The High Court injunction provoked a huge outcry both within Ireland and internationally. 7,000 people marched in protest to the Dáil, radio phone-in programmes were inundated with calls, newspapers were deluged with letters expressing both anti-abortion and pro-choice points of view, and many points between. For several weeks, the Irish national media focused on the case to the near-total exclusion of other news items. Ireland was riveted by its own barbarism. The international media covered the 'story' widely (and sometimes wildly), representing the country as 'backward', 'barbarous', 'misogynistic', 'punitive', 'priest-ridden' and so on and on.

Ireland's growing international reputation for what was repeatedly referred to as 'Ceaucescu-style' government did not please our political leaders, for whom markets are at least as important as morals. The Government applied intense pressure on the girl's family to appeal the High Court judgement to the Supreme Court, with the Government undertaking to pay all expenses. The family eventually agreed and the appeal was heard on 24, 25 and 26 February 1992 by the five male judges of the Supreme Court: Chief Justice Thomas Finlay, Mr Justice Niall McCarthy, Mr Justice Hugh O'Flaherty, Mr Justice Anthony Hederman, Mr Justice Seamus Egan.

Before issuing the text of its ruling to the media, the Supreme Court publicly declared that it was lifting the injunction. The fourteen-year-old rape victim and her

12

parents were free to travel outside the jurisdiction. They returned to the UK where she obtained an abortion, thus finally freeing her from the appalling rack of anguish on which she must have suffered throughout this disgraceful legal and judicial débâcle.

Although the outcry then abated somewhat, it resurfaced when the Supreme Court judges released their full judgement on 5 March. Extraordinarily, in the face of the 1983 anti-abortion amendment which, in the minds of the electorate, the legislators and the Catholic Church, had enforced a complete ban on abortion in Ireland, the majority ruling of the Supreme Court was that abortion was lawful in Ireland in the event of there being 'a real and substantial risk to the life, as distinct from the health, of the mother', as in the case of a threatened suicide. The concept of the equal right to life of 'mother' and foetus enshrined in the Constitution had given way to a superior right to life for the pregnant woman in certain, admittedly highly restricted, circumstances.

This completely unexpected outcome of the judgment raised the immediate and virulently expressed ire of Ireland's strong anti-abortion lobby who demanded that the Supreme Court judgement be overturned by the 'will of the people', through another referendum which would reinstate the 'original meaning' of the Eighth Amendment.

In fact, the Supreme Court ruling left crucial issues still undetermined. For example, it did not clarify the precise conditions under which abortion could be lawful in Ireland, nor who might determine the validity of those conditions. Who, for example, would be entitled to validate a threat of suicide? What exactly was meant by a 'real and substantial risk' to the life of the mother? Two of the judges seemed to disagree on the interpretation of the Offences Against the Person Act, 1861, with Justice McCarthy arguing that under the terms of this Act abortion was always unlawful while Justice Egan argued, in respect of the same Act, that not all abortion would be considered as unlawful.

The court actually rapped the legislature sharply over its collective knuckles for having failed to legislate on the matter of abortion following the 1983 Amendment:

> It is not for the courts to programme society; that is partly, at least, the role of the legislature. The courts are not equipped to regulate these procedures. [...] The failure by the legislature to enact the appropriate legislation is no longer just unfortunate, it is inexcusable. What are pregnant women to do? What are the parents of a pregnant girl under age to do? What are doctors to do? (Justice McCarthy, Judgement: *Attorney General v X and Others*)

This is an especially significant judicial comment since it cuts across one of the most consistently and strongly reiterated feminist arguments both during the campaign to amend the Constitution and subsequently. Feminists in Ireland have repeatedly stressed the unsuitability of the Constitution in particular and of an adversarial legal system more generally as solutions to the 'problem' of reproductive freedom:

> Casting the law as central to the abortion debate will not produce solutions. A much more expansive concept of what pregnancy means is required to effect an enduring reconciliation of the interest of the woman and the unborn. And the debate needs further to be broadened to encompass related issues - including the incidence of rape and sexual abuse, and the whole nature of sexuality ...[10]

Elsewhere too feminists have urged resistance to 'the move towards more law and the creeping hegemony of the legal order'.[11] The unreliability of the law as a basis for the expansion of women's reproductive freedom is all too clear in the USA at present, where the Constitutional guarantee of privacy with regard to abortion is now under serious threat with the challenge to *Roe v Wade*.

Act 2: The Right to Travel and Information

The Supreme Court did not rule conclusively on the right of pregnant women to travel abroad to obtain an abortion. In their *obiter dicta*, or non-binding asides, three of the five justices held that the right to travel was subordinate to the right to life. This means, in effect, that while a woman is entitled to travel abroad for an abortion - may indeed be entitled to obtain a lawful abortion in Ireland - if there is a 'real and substantial risk' to her life, a pregnant woman in any other circumstances does not necessarily have the right to travel abroad to terminate her pregnancy.

This contradictory situation is by no means the end of the endless farce in the matter of judgements. The situation had become far more complicated during the 1980s. In 1985, SPUC (the Society for the Protection of the Unborn Child) initiated a legal action against the two major pregnancy counselling services for women in Ireland, Open Line Counselling and the Dublin Well Woman Centre. SPUC maintained that the provision of a non-directive counselling service was in violation of Article 40.3.3 of the Constitution. In 1986, the High Court placed an injunction on both services, and the Well Woman Centre ceased its counselling service.

An appeal to the Supreme Court by both services in 1988 failed to reverse the High Court decision. The Supreme Court judgement specifically prohibited the centres from giving pregnant women, seeking abortion, the names, addresses or telephone numbers of clinics abroad. Since then, the Well Woman Centre has provided a non-directive counselling service without being able to provide specific information about abortion services.

The centres subsequently brought the case to the European Commission of Human Rights which held, in a preliminary ruling, that Ireland was in violation of Article 10 of the European Convention (the right to receive and impart information). The case went before the full court in March 1992 and the definitive ruling is expected to be given within the coming months.[12]

In yet another 'information' case, known as *Grogan*, in 1989, SPUC sought an injunction in the High Court preventing the officers (fourteen in all) of the Union of Students in Ireland (USI) from publishing information about abortion services.[13] Justice Mella Carroll (then the only woman justice in the High Court) referred the case for adjudication to the European Court of Justice (ECJ) in Luxembourg. Later that same year, the (all male) Supreme Court upheld an appeal brought by SPUC, although it did not rule on the questions referred by Justice Carroll to the ECJ. In 1991, the ECJ ruled that:

It is not contrary to Community law for a member state in which medical termination of pregnancy is forbidden to prohibit students' associations from distributing information about the identity and location of clinics in another member state where voluntary termination of pregnancy is lawfully carried out and the means of communicating with those clinics, where the clinics in question have no involvement in the distribution of the said information.

However, the European court did not rule on the legality of the prohibition on the distribution of information in all cases: its ruling referred specifically to the dissemination of information by 'students' associations'. In fact, the court also ruled that abortion is a service 'within the Treaty of Rome'.

SPUC subsequently sought a further hearing in the High Court to obtain a permanent order restraining the students from distributing information and this case is due to be heard in July 1992.[14]

In the wake of this deadly carousel of legal harassment by the Pro-Life forces, RTE (*the national broadcasting station*) forbade any live discussion of abortion on radio or TV (the ban was subsequently lifted). As recently as six months ago, books such as *Our Bodies Ourselves* and even the British telephone directories were removed from the shelves of Irish public libraries. They were removed because they contained information (ie names, addresses and telephone numbers) of abortion clinics in Britain. The books were subsequently replaced although, as in Wonderland, they are no doubt liable to 'be disappeared' again at any moment.

The construction (destruction) of 'woman' which emerges overwhelmingly from these and other statements by both the male judiciary and the (even more male) Catholic Church leaders is of a subordinate being (hardly a 'citizen'), morally irresponsible and intellectually unreliable, whose 'agency', in so far as she is allowed agency at all, requires to be controlled by the (patriarchal) state for the 'greater good'. Women's citizenship rights - to information, or to freedom of movement and of expression for example - may be curtailed or withdrawn at the whim of theological argument, judicial interpretation, political protocol or some other patriarchal strategy. Women are not 'persons' (moral agents and/or citizens); they are reduced to reproductive or sexual functions.[15]

Act 3: The Maastricht Treaty and the Irish Protocol

About the time of the Supreme Court ruling in the case of X, a further extraordinary complication to this sorry business emerged. It transpired that in December 1991, as the final draft of the Maastricht Treaty was being drawn up, the Irish Government had requested the insertion of a Protocol which would guarantee that the EC would not interfere with Article 40.3.3 of the Constitution.

Clearly, the Protocol was an attempt to ensure that Ireland would not be 'polluted' by the stench of reality - by abortion. Abortions needed by flesh-and-blood Irish women, for all kinds of reasons, at all stages of their childbearing lives, from all over the country, from all social classes.

The Protocol sought to ensure that abortion could never be introduced in Ireland as a consequence of our membership of the EC. It sought to ensure that Ireland could continue to deny the blunt reality of thousands of Irish women travelling to Britain every year.

Even from the most conservative perspective, there was no need for this extraordinary Protocol. The Offences Against the Person Act, 1861 is still on the Statute books. The Act designates abortion or the procuring of an abortion as criminal offences. Article 40.3.3 is still in place. The Supreme Court had ruled that there was no right to information which could be seen as helping to procure an abortion. The EC has no policy in relation to abortion and is not developing such a policy. There is no threat to Irish law from that quarter.

The European Court of Justice had indeed determined that abortion is a 'service' and that EC citizens (including Irish citizens) could be argued to have a right to avail themselves of this service (and many others) in other EC member states. However, as we have seen, when this matter came before the High Court in the case of the *Attorney General v X and Others*, Justice Costello ruled that the right to travel to another EC member state for the purposes of procuring an abortion would be subjected to

17

the provisions of the right to life of the unborn on the grounds that the EC allows derogations for reasons of 'public policy' in member states.

Given the protections afforded the foetus by the Constitution and Statute law in Ireland (which, from a woman-centred perspective are severe restrictions, amounting to absolute prohibitions, placed on Irish women, preventing them from exercising reproductive freedom), it seems that the insertion of the Protocol in the Maastricht Treaty was a political strategy made by the Government under pressure from extreme right-wing anti-abortion forces. Far from serving any necessary or useful legal purpose (ie in clarifying the relation of Irish and EC law with regard to abortion), the Protocol actually complicated the issue beyond belief.

One of the more alarming aspects of this farce is that had the case of X not come before the courts when it did in February, it is probable that the electorate would have remained in complete ignorance of the implications of the Protocol. How the Government would eventually have presented the Protocol to the electorate without the publicity surrounding the X case must remain forever a mystery. But it is not stretching the bounds of credibility, given the chaotic antics of the past months, to express serious reservations about the comprehensiveness, accuracy and reliability of the information the Irish electorate would have received.

Whatever the Government's intentions (which were at best confused), the discovery of the Protocol caused uproar in Ireland. Pregnant women would be prevented from travelling abroad for abortions, from obtaining information about abortion and, most disturbingly, they would have no right of legal recourse to the European Court of Justice with regard to abortion. The Irish state and the now extremely unclear and basically unworkable Article 40.3.3 would rule supreme and unthwarted. A campaign group, composed of feminist activists from diverse strands of the women's movement and other left-wing activists, formed rapidly to demand (1) the withdrawal of the Maastricht Protocol, (2) the introduction of legislation to provide services in specific circumstances (in accordance with the X case Supreme Court judgement), and (3) ultimately, the repeal of Article 40.3.3, primary source of the denial of women's rights to travel, information and abortion.

Arguing that the Protocol 'creates a separate group of European citizens with fewer rights and without the guarantee of protection by the European courts', the Repeal the Eighth Amendment Campaign stressed the high degree of legal uncertainty over the exact relation of Irish and European law and the continuing threat of injunctions against pregnant women seeking abortions abroad. Calling for the repeal of the Eighth Amendment (ie Article 40.3.3), the Campaign statement declared:

The Eighth Amendment is inhumane and unworkable ... [It] allows no exceptions in cases of rape, incest, severe deformity of the foetus, or of a threat to the health of a pregnant woman. The amendment provides for only one exception in a case where the life of a woman is medically shown to be under severe threat. This leaves pregnant young girls, victims of incest, HIV-positive pregnant women, and pregnant women whose physical or mental well-being may be undermined by bringing the pregnancy to term without choices or the means to implement some of those choices in Ireland. [...] This campaign asserts that the bodily integrity, freedom of movement, health and dignity of Irish women can never be guaranteed so long as the right to life of a pregnant woman is equated (in the Constitution) with that of the foetus she is carrying. The rights of pregnant women must be strengthened, based on information and choice.[16]

With party political support coming from the small Democratic Left and the even smaller Green Party, scarce human and financial resources and relentless opposition from a Government intent on 'selling' Maastricht to the electorate at any price, it is hardly surprising that the Campaign did not succeed in exerting sufficient pressure to have the Protocol withdrawn.

Under duress, the Government eventually returned to Europe and obtained a Solemn Declaration, now appended to the Protocol and which purports to reduce its effect. However, in the opinion of many Irish and European lawyers, the Solemn Declaration, has no binding status in European law and is no more than a rhetorical gesture.

The Government has now said it will hold a further referendum in November 1992 to address the issues of travel and information and - responding to pressure from the fundamentalist right - has not ruled out the possibility of a referendum on what it calls the 'substantive issue', the code phrase for the unmentionable, ie legal abortion. However, the Government has refused so far to publish the wording of this referendum or referenda, simply appealing to voters and to women in particular to 'trust us'. Why women should or would trust an almost entirely male Government which has so far either actively obstructed women's struggle for reproductive freedom or entirely ignored the fact that women do happen to reproduce (by failing to provide childcare services, for example), is entirely mysterious to me.

Given the strength and oft-proven capacity of the anti-abortion movement to exert pressure at the highest level, both in Ireland and elsewhere, there are well-grounded fears that the Government will either delay or renege on its various (and confused) undertakings with regard to the issues of travel and information. And there is the awful possibility that an even more draconian amendment to the Constitution may be proposed and carried by a confused electorate always susceptible to emotional manipulation by Pro-Life discourse and still capable of being swayed by the subtly intimidatory tactics of the Catholic Church.

Two thirds of the electorate have declared in recent polls that they are in favour of the introduction of abortion services in limited circumstances in Ireland. While this is a dramatic advance on the previously stark 'No' position of 1983, there is a long way to go between now (June) and November. Half-way to the divorce referendum held in 1986, the electorate changed its mind and, having indicated majority openness to the introduction of divorce, it then voted against it.

Epilogue: About Facts and Feminism
Officially, 4,000 Irish women, unofficially probably closer to 7,000 or 8,000 women, travel to Britain for abortions every year. Since 1983, a minimum of 36,000 women, and probably closer to 70,000, have made the journey. They go

to Britain because they have no choice. And they go to Britain without the vital information which is their right and possibly their only comfort.

These women are forced to go abroad because their needs and their rights are denied by the Irish Constitution, by Irish Statute law and by Irish social provisions. Ireland and its legislators behave as if women's needs do not count and do not even exist. Quite literally, Irish women obtaining abortions in Britain are not counted in the Irish census. Women's real life needs do not suit the image of Ireland preferred by our legislators and by our religious police so they effectively deny the very existence of those who do not fit. If it's not visible, it's not there. Women having abortions do not exist so their needs do not have to be met.

Throughout this century and up until the early 1960s, it was the practice in Ireland for single women who 'became' pregnant (ie, women who were impregnated by men) to be confined to convents where they did laundry work and other such hard labour for the duration of their pregnancy and beyond. They were obliged to give up their 'illegitimate' children for adoption. Women who bore children outside marriage were not just stigmatised, they were treated like toxic waste and buried alive. The plainest fact of women's biology, that a marriage certificate is not a precondition of pregnancy, was simply denied. The facts of women's lives didn't fit the image so women were locked away. Out of sight, out of mind.

Which is precisely how Ireland has continued to behave into the 1990s. Britain, ironically, has become a vast laundry for the human 'dirty linen' that Irish morality refuses to handle.

While I have not focused here on the complex roots and motivations of the anti-abortion movement in Ireland, it is of the utmost importance to emphasise its close links with the Catholic Church and its apparently unlimited access to parliamentary legislators.[17] As in the USA and elsewhere, they are a highly organised, well-funded and largely secret pressure group who do not hesitate to use the most sinister tactics in seeking to conserve the moral 'purity' of Ireland, bastion of conservative Catholicism in the western world. They are prepared to pay any price to achieve their objective. The Catholic Church in Ireland has developed a foetocentric rhetoric and ethics from which any acknowledgement of the needs of pregnant women has been exorcised. Women, after all, are the devil itself. During the X case, Church leaders did not once express concern at this girl's plight, nor has it done so for the thousands of women obtaining abortions every year. There has been no attempt whatsoever on the part of either Church or political leaders to examine the reasons for the high rates of abortion in (yet paradoxically not 'in') Ireland. Women are forced to travel in shameful secrecy, treated with contempt by a scandalously irresponsible leadership. The right to control women's bodies absolutely is assumed without question by the hegemonically male religious and political hierarchies.

In this context, it has been difficult for Irish feminists to develop a high profile, pro-active, firmly pro-choice politics. Feminists are constantly placed in a reactive position, seeking to prevent the further erosion of women's rights and to fend off the ubiquitous menace of the Church-inspired fundamentalists. Nonetheless, and often at high personal cost, Irish feminists have persisted in asserting women's right to reproductive freedom.[18]

In April, 220 women of all ages and backgrounds, with variously assorted children, set off by boat from Dublin to Wales under the banner of the 'Women's Coalition'. We wanted to express our sense of anger at what had happened to one fourteen-year-old girl whose case we knew of, as well as our support and solidarity with the many thousands of women who have made that sad trip anonymously over so many years. It was called 'The Sister Ship'.

At present, a strong core of Irish feminists are campaigning against the Maastricht Treaty with its anti-woman Protocol, and preparing for the long lead-in to another divisive 'abortion' referendum. We are determined that women will no longer have to travel abroad in shame and fear, denied their rights to information and to legal abortion in Ireland, or elsewhere.

The sadistic farce must cease.

Ailbhe Smyth
June 1992

Notes

1. Although Ireland has a woman President, Mary Robinson, elected in 1990, women constitute only 7.8 per cent of the Dáil (Irish Parliament). There are 166 male deputies and thirteen female deputies.
2. The *Constitution of Ireland* (1937) is precise about the confinement of women. Article 41.2 states:
   1. In particular, the State recognises that by her life within the home, woman gives to the State a support without which the common good cannot be achieved.
   2. The State shall, therefore, endeavour to ensure that mothers shall not be obliged by economic necessity to engage in labour to the neglect of their duties in the home.
   Women are named directly as a social group only in Article 41, which deals with 'The Family', in the non-binding Article 45 on 'Directive Principles of Social Policy', and in Article 40.3.3
3. The Council for the Status of Women is an independent, although state-funded, grouping of approximately eighty women's organisations and groups in the Republic of Ireland. Pauline Conroy Jackson has argued that Ireland has 'the best organised institutional movement of women in Europe' (Communication to the meeting held in the Mansion House, Dublin, to discuss 'Women and Maastricht', 29 April 1992)
4. Frances Fitzgerald: Address to Annual Conference of the Council for the Status of Women, Dublin, 4 April 1992.
5. I am indebted to Lia Mills for suggesting the concept of 'half-life'.
6. Whatever the circumstances, under Irish law anyone having sexual intercourse with a minor is guilty of 'statutory rape'.
7. Emily O'Reilly gives a precise chronology of the events in the case of X in her analysis of the rise of the Catholic fundamentalist right in Ireland: *Masterminds of the Right*. I am indebted to this acute and detailed study for many factual aspects of my article.
8. Pauline Conroy Jackson, 29 April 1992.
9. Emily O'Reilly, p132.
10. Marie Fox and Therese Murphy: 'If Men got Pregnant ...' *Fortnight Magazine*, No. 305, April 1992, Belfast.
11. Carol Smart (1989): *Feminism and the Power of the Law*
12. Information supplied by the Dublin Well Woman Centre.
13. The students were represented in the High Court by Mary Robinson, then a senior counsel. The case was subsequently taken over by former Attorney General, John Rogers, following Mary Robinson's election as President of Ireland in 1990.
14. SPUC was granted a permanent injunction by the High Court on 8 August 1992, restraining fourteen students' union officers from distributing information on abortion clinics abroad. Mr Justice Morris also ordered that the papers in the case should be sent to the Director of Public Prosecutions so

that he could consider whether the defendants (ie the students' union officers) should be prosecuted for contempt of court (*The Irish Times*, 9/8/92). The students have since declared their intention of continuing to distribute information and of going to prison if necessary (*Ed. July 1992*).

15. These and other points are strongly argued by Attracta Ingram elsewhere in this volume. In addition, three Irish feminists have recently addressed a Petition to the European Parliament, formally complaining of the 'Government of Ireland's failure to provide for: their right to free movement as citizens, to travel without discrimination in relation to their sex and to travel to avail of lawful services in Member States of the European Community' (Dublin, 5 April 1992).

16. Repeal the Eighth Amendment Campaign statement, Dublin, 14 April 1992.

17. But see Emily O'Reilly, *Masterminds of the Right*, for a full account of their connections and machinations.

18. For an excellent account of Irish feminist resistance to the 1983 referendum see Ursula Barry: 'Abortion in the Republic of Ireland', 1988.

Abortion Law in Ireland after the Maastricht Referendum

Introduction

The legal position in Ireland about abortion itself, information on abortion and travelling abroad for abortion is complicated by the fact that three different legal systems - Irish Constitutional law, European Community law, and the European Convention on Human Rights - influence Irish law in this area. Each of these three systems has a different approach to the issues, operates by different rules and procedures, and may be interpreted by different courts. Their relationships with each other are subtle and complicated, causing controversy even between experts.[1] Moreover, this area of the law is developing rapidly, with a host of new judgments, interpretations, emerging problems and inconsistencies further muddying the waters during the first six months of 1992.

What European Community law rights are still available to Irish women following ratification of the Maastricht Protocol? What will be the effects in Ireland of the European Court of Human Rights' decision later in 1992 on the ban against Irish clinics providing abortion information? Does the Constitution itself restrict the changes that can be made to Article 40.3.3 in the forthcoming referendum?

I propose to start by looking at Irish Constitutional law, then at European Community law and the European Convention on Human Rights as they affected Irish law until the referendum on 18 June 1992, and next at how the ratification of the Maastricht Protocol changes the picture in Ireland. Finally, I want to explore briefly what legal parameters constrain the debate on proposed wordings for a new referendum on abortion issues.

Irish Constitutional Law

Irish Constitutional law on abortion issues is dominated by Article 40.3.3, inserted in 1983, which provides that:

The state acknowledges the right to life of the unborn, and with due regard to the equal right to life of the mother, guarantees in its laws to respect and, as far as practicable, by its laws to defend and vindicate that right.

Before Art 40.3.3, distributing material 'advocating abortion' had been technically illegal under the Censorship of Publications Act but this dealt primarily with printed material and did not affect verbal individual counselling. In *Open Door Counselling*[2], the courts found that nondirective pregnancy counselling was unlawful under Art 40.3.3 and gave a permanent injunction against the clinics concerned resuming it; the High Court suggested that it could also be a criminal offence under the old common-law heading of 'conspiracy to corrupt public morals'.[3] *Grogan*[4] clarified that this prohibition also extended to distributing addresses and phone numbers of British clinics, without a counselling element. Although the Irish Constitution gives citizens rights to freedom of expression and an implied right to information, the courts held that in both cases these rights were subordinate to the right to life of the foetus under Art 40.3.3 as a more basic human right.

In X,[5] the court examined the situation of women who wanted to travel to Britain for abortions which were legal there. This had never been thought illegal before in Ireland, as criminal law does not normally have effect outside the jurisdiction. Here, however, the High Court issued an injunction against a pregnant girl who intended to go to Britain for an abortion. The Supreme Court overruled the judge's decision on the facts of the case, but it too decided by a 3:2 majority that women who expressed the intention of going abroad for an abortion could be prevented from leaving the country. Although two judges disagreed strongly with this idea, the other three thought that the implicit right to travel which the Constitution confers on Irish citizens was subordinate to the courts' duty to protect the right to life of the foetus.

It is worth noting that the courts have said they would feel compelled to restrict information and travel concerned with abortion, even if women's health might be adversely affected and abortions would not be effectively prevented.[6]

The courts' obligations to prevent abortion had been described in very forceful terms in these judgements. For example, Hamilton P said in *Open Door*: 'As I have already stated that right to life [of the unborn] includes the right to have that right preserved and defended and to be guarded against all threats to its existence before and after birth, and that it lies not in the power of a parent to terminate its existence and that any action on the part of any person endangering that life was necessarily not only an offence against the common good but also against the guaranteed personal rights of the human life in question.'[7]

However, until recently these pronouncements were made in general terms and no case dealt with a specific situation where a woman wanted to have an abortion. Under section 58 of the Offences Against the Person Act, 1861, still in force in Ireland, any person who 'with intent to procure the miscarriage of any woman, whether she be or be not with child, shall unlawfully administer to her or cause to be taken by her any poison or noxious thing, or shall unlawfully use any instrument or other means whatsoever with the like intent, shall be guilty of felony'.

In the *Attorney General v X & Others*, the Supreme Court delivered what one legal commentator described as a 'bombshell'[8] by deciding that under Art 40.3.3 not all abortions were illegal in Ireland. However, the departure was not as radical as some authorities suggested. The wording of Art 40.3.3 had always suggested that the rights of the foetus were not absolute where the mother's life was under threat. Those abortions acceptable to Catholic theology under the doctrine of 'indirect intent', such as in cases of ectopic pregnancy, had been widely known to be performed in Irish hospitals for many years. In delivering judgement in *Open Door Counselling*, which found abortion information and counselling illegal, the High Court had specifically stated that it was not dealing with a situation where the 'equal right to life of the mother' described in Art 40.3.3 might be at risk.[9]

All five Supreme Court judges in X decided that Art 40.3.3 sanctioned abortion in the cases where the pregnancy probably constitutes a 'real and substantive risk to the life as distinct from the health of the mother, which can only be avoided by the termination of the pregnancy'. The risk need not be immediate, ie, the doctor need not wait until the mother is at the point of death to perform the operation. This ground was not a wide one; the controversial feature of the judgement was their decision by a 4:1 majority that a fourteen-year-old girl, pregnant reportedly due to rape, who was thought likely to commit suicide if she was prevented from having an abortion, came within its terms.

European Community Law
European Community law is binding in Ireland on terms laid down by the EC Treaties and according to Art 29.4 of the Constitution it also overrides any other provision of the Constitution which conflicts with it. Insofar as Community law relates to abortion, therefore, its provisions have superior force in Ireland to the Irish Constitution.

There are some important practical limitations on this rule. Firstly, it depends upon a co-operative relationship between the Irish courts and the European Court of Justice (ECJ) in Luxembourg, which is the supreme court of Community law. The usual method of communication between Irish courts and the ECJ is the reference procedure, whereby the Irish court, identifying a possible point of Community law in the case before it, can ask the ECJ to give it a formal interpretation on the Community law issue. Usually, whether to ask the ECJ for a ruling is a matter for the Irish judge's discretion; but the last court of appeal in Ireland is obliged under Community law to refer to the ECJ if either party to the case so requests. However, Irish courts have been slow to refer points to do with the specific issue of abortion. The Supreme Court refused to refer in *Open Door*, despite its obligation to do so as the final court of appeal, on very strained reasoning, and was very critical of Carroll J's decision to refer the *Grogan* case.[10] Secondly, the ECJ's heavy workload makes it very slow; it normally takes eighteen months and more to get the ECJ's decision. This delay causes obvious problems in relation to cases involving abortion.

Community law's relevance to abortion is limited. Its main preoccupation is with the economic law of the market, and not with social, moral or health issues; it sees these as remaining a matter for the individual state. Whether or not abortion is legal in Ireland is not affected by Community law and no change in this approach is foreseeable.[11]

A distinction arises, however, in relation to restrictions on travel to, or information about, abortion facilities in other member states. Community law is concerned with free movement of economic services between member states. The ECJ was asked to look at this aspect in *Grogan*,[12] the case concerning students' unions which distributed in Ireland details of abortion clinics in Britain. In a complex judgement, the court reaffirmed that Irish laws banning abortion were not within the scope of Community law. However, it held that the medical termination of pregnancy was an economic service within the meaning of the EC Treaty. This means, according to the court's other caselaw, that abortion clinics from other member states would have a Community law right to advertise their services in Ireland, and Irish citizens would have a Community law right to receive that information. Irish women would also have a right under Community law to travel to other member states for abortions.[13] However, the students were third parties who had no economic interest in the matter, and the ECJ therefore held that they had no Community law right to distribute information.

If the case had involved a plaintiff who was entitled to Community law rights under the principle of free movement of services, such as for example an Irish woman prevented from travelling for an abortion, or a British abortion clinic prevented from advertising in Ireland, would their Community law rights have outweighed the conflicting requirements of Irish law?

The balance between the authority of member states and the ECJ in this situation is complicated. Community caselaw may entitle the member state to restrict rights arising from freedom of movement, on grounds of important public policy,[14] and this normally gives the member state a wide margin of discretion. So far, however, the public policy derogation has only been claimed by the state where the service was based, and it is not clear whether the ECJ would extend it to a state trying to keep out services based in another country.[15]

If Irish law can benefit from this derogation, it still has another hurdle to overcome. Recent developments in Community caselaw, particularly the *ERT* case,[16] show that if a member state chooses to restrict an important Community principle such as free movement of services, on the grounds of public policy, the ECJ may still find the state's measures illegal if it considers they infringe fundamental rights recognised by the Community, or are disproportionate to the aim they try to achieve, or unnecessary to that aim.[17] Commentators agree that the fundamental right to life given to the unborn would be accepted by the ECJ as a genuine public policy issue in Ireland, but both Curtin and Hogan doubt whether the ECJ would see preventing pregnant women leaving the country as necessary or proportionate in this context.[18] AG van Gerven in *Grogan* specifically stated that 'measures which would be disproportionate - inasmuch as they would excessively impede the freedom to provide services - would include, for example, a ban on pregnant women going abroad or a rule under which they would be subject to unsolicited examinations upon their return from abroad.'[19]

In summary, then, while Community law has no relevance to whether abortion is available in Ireland or not, there is a strong possibility that it does give enforceable rights to Irish women both to travel to other member states for abortion and to receive in Ireland information provided by commercial abortion clinics abroad or their agents. It does not protect non-directive counselling or the distribution of information by disinterested third parties. However, the Irish courts will shortly be deciding the *Grogan* case on the basis of the ECJ's decision, and their judgements may throw further light on this point.

The European Convention on Human Rights

Unlike Community law, the European Convention on Human Rights has no force within Ireland. Irish citizens can take cases to its court, the European Court of Human Rights (ECHR) in Strasbourg, against the Irish Government, but the court's findings cannot be enforced in Irish law and its caselaw is not binding on Irish courts. The Irish Government is supposed to take action to remedy legislation which the Strasbourg court finds in breach of the Convention, but in practice this is often long-delayed (as for example in the *Norris* case).

A recent development, however, is the increased reliance of the ECJ on the caselaw of the Convention to help it in defining fundamental rights in Community law.[20] Thus, for instance, the concept of proportionality in Community law mentioned above draws partly on the same concept in the caselaw of the ECHR.

In relation to the availability of abortion in Ireland, the Convention does not recognise an absolute right to life for the foetus itself, nor any specific right to abortion, but accepts a wide variation in member states' approaches to this issue. There is a right to travel in Art 2(2) of the Convention, but it only extends to leaving your own country and states may limit it on several grounds including public morality and public policy; so Irish law is unlikely to contravene it.[21]

The *Open Door Counselling* case presently before the ECHR deals with the ban on clinics counselling or informing women about the availability of abortion abroad. This was argued to contravene Art 10 of the Convention which provides a right to freedom of information. The report of the Commission on Human Rights (usually an indication of how the court will rule) issued on 7 March 1991: the full hearing before the court took place on 24 March 1992[22] and their judgment is expected to issue in autumn.

The Commission found[23] by an 8:5 majority that the ban violated Art 10 of the Convention insofar as it prevented the applicant clinics from providing information. The reasoning here was quite narrow; the Commission thought that the law had been too unclear and unpredictable for the clinics to have realised in advance that their counselling activities were unlawful. (This might not apply to any other plaintiff, who would have been well aware of the ban after the first *Open Door* decision.) Most Commissioners did not examine any deeper issues after finding in the clinics' favour on this point. However, the Commission very importantly also held by a 7:6 majority that the ban violated the right to freedom of information of two individual women (not pregnant at the time but of childbearing age), by denying them access to relevant services. Three other commissioners also added that even if the laws had been foreseeable, they exceeded what was necessary in a democratic society. They argued that the ban adversely affected women's health (because they sought abortions later and did not return for the recommended check-up six weeks afterwards), and were a considerable interference with freedom of expression, but appeared quite ineffective to prevent abortions taking place. If the Court of Human Rights follows the Commission's approach, as seems likely, the Government will be obliged under the Convention to amend the law to remove the possibility of such a ban. It may or may not choose to do so immediately. More importantly, the view of the ECHR would be a very influential factor in any future decision by the ECJ in adjudicating whether Irish measures which restricted freedom of movement in Community law were permissible public policy exceptions at the member state's discretion, or were unacceptable because they infringed fundamental rights.

The Effects of the Maastricht Protocol

On 18 June 1992, the Irish people voted by referendum to ratify the Maastricht Treaty, supplementing and modifying the European Community Treaties. It includes Protocol 17, inserted by the Irish Government, which provides that:

Nothing in the Treaty on European Union, or in the Treaties establishing the European Communities, or in the Treaties or Acts modifying or supplementing those Treaties, shall affect the application in Ireland of Article 40.3.3 of the Constitution of Ireland.

Technically, a question still hangs over the Maastricht Treaty ever coming into force, as the Community still has to sort out the difficult problems resulting from Denmark's rejection of the Treaty. It appears probable at the time of writing that sheer political determination will result in a legal solution being cobbled together by the remaining member states with Danish agreement. At present, it seems unlikely that it will be feasible for Ireland to further complicate the scenario by deleting its Protocol, a step which would require re-ratification in all the other member states. Due to constraints of space, I am dealing with the question here on the basis that the substance of the Maastricht Protocol will come into force in Ireland following ratification by the other member states, although it is not yet clear when that will be.

On the face of it, the Protocol's effect is to remove the overriding force of Community law over Art 40.3.3 of the Constitution. The law on availability of abortion in Ireland, which is not affected by Community law, would remain unchanged. The position in relation to travel and information in Irish law at present would, however, change substantially. Irish women could not after all seek to assert a Community law right to travel to other member states for abortion or to receive information about abortion services available there, as suggested by the ECJ's judgment in *Grogan*. The practical effect of the ECHR caselaw on rights to information, through its influence on Community caselaw, would also be curtailed.

Some authorities[24] have suggested that this is an over-simple reading and that the words 'application in Ireland' in the Protocol mean that it could not be used in relation to travel outside Ireland or information about activities abroad. However, this seems unconvincing. The receipt of information, the distribution of abortion advertising, the making of an injunction against travel, clearly take place within Ireland.[25] Hamilton P in *Open Door* refused a reference to the ECJ by holding that the counselling agencies' activities took place in Ireland. A possible exception is an Irish woman who had already left the country for an abortion before an injunction was made, but the action for damages against her which is contemplated *obiter* in *Open Door*[26] could still take place in Ireland after her return.

The Solemn Declaration negotiated by the Irish Government on the interpretation of the Protocol, and signed on 1 May 1992, provides that member states agree:

That it was and is their intention that the Protocol shall not limit freedom either to travel between member States, or, in accordance with conditions which may be laid down in conformity with Community law, by Irish legislation, to obtain or make available in Ireland, information relating to services legally available in other Member States. At the same time the High Contracting Parties solemnly declare that in the event of a future constitutional amendment in Ireland which concerns the subject-matter of Article 40.3.3 of the Constitution of Ireland and which does not conflict with the intention of the High Contracting Parties hereinbefore expressed, they will, following the entry into force of the Treaty on European Union, be favourably disposed to amending the said Protocol so as to extend its application to such constitutional amendment if Ireland so requests.

There has been considerable debate about the legal force of the Declaration, particularly in view of the fact that the specific intention of at least the Irish Government when the Protocol was signed appears, on the contrary, to have been that the Community law rights foreshadowed in the *Grogan* decision should not come into force in Ireland.[27] The balance of opinion is that the Declaration is not binding,[28] although there are expert opinions to the contrary.[29]

It was suggested at first that the ECJ might declare the Protocol invalid because it interfered with Community rights to which Irish citizens were already entitled.[30] However, it seems doubtful whether the ECJ has the power to invalidate what will at that stage be an integral part of a Community treaty.[31] It is certainly likely that the ECJ would interpret the Protocol as restrictively as possible.[32] However, it may not get the opportunity to do so; given the reluctance shown by Irish courts to permit references to the ECJ on abortion-related issues when the supremacy of Community law in this area was unquestioned, they may well decline references in this area altogether once the Protocol (which can be interpreted by an Irish court) states that Community law is now excluded from supremacy over Art 40.3.3.

Parameters for Changes in Irish Law

Given that the Protocol may well have the effect of insulating Art 40.3.3 from any rights available to Irish women under Community law when the Maastricht Treaty comes into effect, and that the Convention on Human Rights has no force inside Ireland, Irish Constitutional law on abortion now appears immune to challenge from any other legal system. It does, however, face the prospect of change from within, with a referendum promised for autumn 1992 on travel and information, and campaigns in progress to hold a second or extended referendum on the availability of abortion in Ireland. Decisions on the content of the referenda are highly charged; but what legal parameters influence their content?

A referendum legitimising travel for abortion abroad appears to be the least controversial politically, being apparently acceptable to sections of the pro-life movement. Following X, travel for an abortion abroad is legal at present where the woman's life is in danger. It seems, following the Declaration, that the Government may intend to reintroduce the equivalent of the Community law right suggested by *Grogan*, which would apply to all Irish women without any requirement of a danger to life. The Community law right, however, would not cover travel to countries other than Community member states (eg the United States) and travel by women who are not Community citizens, and the wording may need to include them specifically. Otherwise this area is fairly uncomplicated and legislation is probably not needed.

The situation in relation to provision of information is much more controversial, with substantial political opposition to relaxing existing controls. Following the X case, however, it is reasonable to assume that the small number of women who are legally entitled to travel for abortions because their lives are at risk, are also entitled to information about that option, and this has been conceded both by the Government[33] and by the Chairman of the

Parliamentary Sub-committee set up to deliberate on the wording.[34] In practice, it would be difficult to restrict information to women who could prove that their lives were at risk. In addition, the Strasbourg Court's judgement in *Open Door* is due in or before autumn 1992, and the Government cannot be seen entirely to neglect its views in wording the referendum. The Government will probably seek to maintain some controls in this area. Other points which need to be dealt with in detail include whether counselling should be treated differently from information, and whether only commercial, or also disinterested agencies, may distribute information. This requires legislation, which will almost certainly have to be referred by the President to the Supreme Court under Art 26 for confirmation that it is in conformity with the Constitution.

The issue of availability of abortion in Ireland is again more controversial. Options include widening its availability to cases of rape or incest, to serious threats to the physical or mental health of the mother, or narrowing it to exclude all cases outside immediate risk to the mother's survival.

One suggestion is the deletion of Art 40.3.3 (favoured by the Council for the Status of Women[35], by the Women's Coalition and by the Repeal the Eighth Amendment Campaign), but it is important to realise that this may not substantially change the present law. Irish Constitutional law on abortion is not confined to Art 40.3.3 itself; a long line of judgements in the Supreme and High Courts have held that a right to life for the foetus is implicit in Irish Constitutional law, before Art 40.3.3 was ever introduced.[36] Deleting Art 40.3.3 would probably not affect the rights of the foetus, though it might be argued to reduce the state's obligation to play an active part in their defence, to which it specifically refers. It would not remove the right to life of the mother, which is guaranteed both explicitly by Art 40.3.2 and implicitly, but it would not necessarily render it more powerful than that of the foetus. Conversely, inserting a more restrictive wording could provide that threats of suicide were not satisfactory evidence that the mother's right to life was threatened, but the Supreme Court cannot in practical terms be excluded from being the ultimate arbiter of whether or not her life is at stake in any given situation.

A referendum to legalise abortion in cases of rape or incest also poses problems. How can it be determined whether the pregnancy results from rape or incest, without holding a court inquiry which might delay the decision until late in the pregnancy? This is another area which would require detailed legislation, probably necessitating corroboration by, at least, medical specialists; here again, the legislation would need to be referred under Art 26, and provisions which the court thought risked permitting abortions where rape could not be verified might be struck down as outside the terms of the referendum.

Finally, the difficult question of time-limits arises. Abortions performed due to risks to the mother's mental or physical health are often subject to time-limits related to the foetus becoming viable. Abortions due to risk to the mother's life usually are not. Should time-limits be placed on these abortions in Ireland? The Supreme Court did not deal with this point in X, where the foetus was clearly not independently viable.

Conclusion

The confusion and inconsistency of abortion law in Ireland seems accurately to reflect a state of flux and uncertainty in public opinion. While conservatives have sought to define an absolute Constitutional right to life for the foetus in all circumstances other than those acceptable to Catholic theology, feminists and liberals have mobilised the resources of European Community law and the Convention on Human Rights to support rights for women to travel abroad for abortions and to reasonable information about abortion services abroad. While the latter stand to lose their force in Irish law when the Maastricht Protocol comes into force, they have nevertheless set the agenda for future referenda on travel and information rights. Meanwhile, the decision in X has appalled conservatives who fear that women may obtain abortions in Ireland by pretending to be suicidal, and appalled feminists by asserting that women may not obtain abortions in Ireland or elsewhere unless they are in danger of death. While it is still unclear whether future referenda will broach the 'substantive issue' of abortion itself, opinion polls in June 1992 suggested that a slim majority of Irish people (64 per cent) would favour extending the grounds for legal abortion to 'special circumstances' including cases of rape and incest, with 17 per cent opposing in all circumstances and 18 per cent restricting to a serious threat to the mother's existence[37]. It remains to be seen how this fragile consensus, which remained stable in polls over May and June 1992, would stand up to the sustained and bitter campaign which is widely feared.

Madeleine Reid
June 1992

Notes

1. See Madeleine Reid, 'The Impact of Community Law in the Irish Constitution', 1990, p81-103; Kingston & Whelan, 'The Protection of the Unborn in 3 Legal Orders', *Irish Law Times*, April 1992.
2. *AG (at the relation of SPUC (Irl) Ltd) v Open Door Counselling Ltd & Dublin Well Woman Centre Ltd*, 1988 IR 593.
3. Ibid, p614.
4. *SPUC (Irl) Ltd v Stephen Grogan & Others*, 1989 IR 753.
5. *AG v X and Others*, Incorporated Council of Law Reporting for Ireland, 1992.
6. Finlay, CJ, in *Open Door*; McCarthy J, in *Grogan*; Finlay, Egan, Hederman, JJ, in *X*.
7. at p617.
8. William Binchy, *The Irish Times*, 27 March 1992.
9. Above, at p617.
10. See Reid, above, p97; similarly Costello J, in *X*, above.
11. See Deirdre Curtin, *The Irish Times*, 2 March 1992, quoted by Gerry Whyte, 'Abortion and the Law', in *Doctrine and Life*, vol 42, no 5, May/June 1992; opinion of AG van Gerven, in *SPUC v Grogan*, Case C-159/90, 1991 2 CEC, at p574.
12. *SPUC v Grogan*, 1991 2 CEC Reports, above.
13. *Luisi & Carbone v Ministero del Tesoro*, 286/82 & 26/83 (1984).
14. See Anthony Collins, 'Commercial Speech and the Free Movement of Goods and Services at Community Law', in *Human Rights and Constitutional Law*, above p328 –, on 3 recent recent cases, *Sager v Dennemeyer* (case C-76/90, judgtt 25/7/91), *Commission v Netherlands*, (case C/53/89, judgtt 25/7/91) and *Stichting Collectieve v Commissariaat voor de Media*, (case C-288/89, judgtt 25/7/91).

15. *Adoni v Belgium*, 1982 ECR 1665: Deirdre Curtin, *The Irish Times*, 14 February 1992; Gerry Hogan, *The Irish Times*, 19 February 1992.
16. *ERT (Elliniki Radiophonia Teleorasi v Dimotiki Etairia Pliroforissis)*, Case C-260/89, Judgement 18/6/91, not yet reported.
17. Francis Jacobs, in *Human Rights and Constitutional Law: essays in honour of Brian Walsh*, ed James O'Reilly, 1992; Reid above, p82-7.
18. Note 15 above.
19. *SPUC v Grogan*, Case C-159/09, 1991 2 CEC at p567.
20. See note 17 above, (Jacobs, Reid).
21. See Kingston & Whelan above.
22. *The Irish Times*, 25 March 1992.
23. 14 European Rights Reports 115, at pp131-152.
24. William Binchy, *The Irish Times*, 25 February 1992.
25. This argument is made in more detail by Gerry Hogan, in *Maastricht and Ireland*, Institute for European Affairs, 1992.
26. At p617.
27. See annotation in Declaration, *Common Market Law Review*, 7 January 1992.
28. William Robinson, in *Doctrine & Life*, above; Gerard Hogan, *The Irish Times*, 17 April 1992.
29. Eoghan Fitzsimons SC, *The Irish Times*, 6 May 1992.
30. Deirdre Curtin, *The Irish Times*, 7 March 1992.
31. See William Robinson above.
32. Curtin, *The Irish Times*, 24 April 1992.
33. During the oral hearing before the Court of Human Rights in *Open Door: The Irish Times*, 25 March 1992.
34. Minister for Justice Padraig Flynn, *The Irish Times*, 27 March 1992.
35. *The Irish Times*, 10 June 1992.
36. Hamilton, *Open Door*, above, at p597; Walsh J, *McGee v Attorney General*, 1974 IR 284 at p310; Walsh, *G v an Bord Uchtála*, 1980 IR 32 at p69; McCarthy J, *Norris v Attorney General*, 1984 IR 36 at p103; O'Flaherty J in *X*, above, at p95
37. *The Irish Times* opinion poll, 10/6/1992; very similar percentages were given in an identical poll in the same paper on 11/5/1992. The figure of 64 per cent is composed of 48 per cent who believed that abortion should be available in 'special circumstances' including rape and incest, and 16 per cent who believed that it should be available on demand.

Abortion: The Case for Legal Reform in Northern Ireland

Abortion Outlawed

The Medical Termination of Pregnancy Bill, the Abortion Act, when introduced to England, Scotland and Wales in 1967, was not extended to Northern Ireland. This Act allows abortions for social and medical reasons and was a great improvement on the pre-existing situation under which an average of 100,000 backstreet abortions were performed yearly.

Because the 1967 Abortion Act was not extended to Northern Ireland, a woman here with an unwanted pregnancy is facing a very difficult situation. She is forced to make one of the following three choices: (1) make an expensive journey to England, where she has to pay privately for the operation; (2) endure her unwanted pregnancy; or (3) have a backstreet abortion.

The present law governing the performance of abortions in Northern Ireland dates back to the nineteenth century and prohibits abortion. The only exception to this is when abortion is necessary to save a woman's life, and it may only be performed after twenty-eight weeks of pregnancy. This anomalous situation was brought about by the 1861 Offences Against the Person Act, which was later amended when the Infant Life Preservation Act was extended to Northern Ireland in 1945.

The 1861 Act provides that: *any person performing, attempting and/or assisting in an abortion ... shall be guilty of felony, and being convicted thereof shall be liable, at the discretion of the court, to be kept in penal servitude for life ...'*

The Infant Life Preservation Act (subtitled, the 'Act to Amend the Law with Regard to Destruction of Children at or before Birth') was passed in England in 1929. This Act does not deal with the first seven months of pregnancy and concerns itself only with the period after the twenty-eighth week of pregnancy up until after birth. It prohibits abortion during this time unless it is necessary to save the woman's life. Because the 1861 Act still covers the period of the first twenty-eight weeks of pregnancy, there is still no legal provision for abortion during this period in Northern Ireland.

The Bourne Judgement

This is exactly the legal situation in which the London gynaecologist Alec Bourne found himself when in 1938 he performed an abortion on a fourteen-year-old victim of multiple rape. Wanting to challenge the ambiguous legal situation, he then presented himself to the police. According to current law the maximum penalty would have been life imprisonment. Bourne pleaded 'not guilty' and submitted that had his client had to endure her pregnancy, she would most certainly have become a psychological wreck. Judge McNaughten accepted the point and explained to the jury that the 1861 Act only prohibits 'unlawful abortions'. If there were unlawful abortions, then Parliament in 1861 must have recognised some abortions to be lawful, he concluded. His interpretation was that all abortions are to be seen as lawful when a doctor is of the opinion that either the woman's life is endangered, or that a continuation of the pregnancy would make the woman a physical or mental wreck.

Judge McNaughten added: 'If the life of the woman can be saved by an operation and a doctor did not perform it because of his religious views, he would be in great peril of being brought before this court on a charge of manslaughter for negligence.'

Doctor Bourne was released, thus showing that the current law was open to interpretation. Although the judgement in the Bourne case was never backed up by a change in the written law, it did at least provide an opening for those doctors who, like Bourne, were willing to perform abortions. However, it was 1967 before the written law was changed to declare emphatically that abortions such as that performed by Bourne in 1938 were lawful.

Legal ambiguity exists in Northern Ireland where the written law forbids abortions, but in practice some are performed. Since the written law as it stands does not cover doctors performing abortions, they certainly try to cover these up by not registering them as such. Therefore it is very hard to get a clear figure on abortions performed in Northern Ireland. Estimates range between 250 and 500 per annum.

The law is so ambiguous that the way in which doctors deal with women seeking an abortion here is inconsistent. Even in extreme cases, such as pregnancy as a result of rape or a severe risk to the health of the woman, there is no guarantee that an abortion will be performed. This demonstrates the urgent need for a change in the law.

As indicated by the amount of women who travel to England for abortions - at least since 1967 - it is clear that in Northern Ireland we are taking advantage of the more liberal situation there. It is hypocritical for people to object to the extension of the 1967 Act to Northern Ireland where it is so obviously needed. The situation at the moment is that we are exporting a problem which we will not face up to ourselves.

The current situation discriminates against Northern Ireland women on two levels: first, against those who must pay an exorbitant amount for an abortion, and second, against those who cannot afford to do this at all and are then left with an unwanted pregnancy or the choice of a backstreet abortion.

The 1967 Abortion Act

The 1967 Abortion Act allows a woman to have a legal abortion when two doctors agree that:

(a) continuing the pregnancy involves a greater risk to her life than an abortion,
(b) continuing the pregnancy involves a greater risk of injury to her physical or mental health than an abortion,
(c) continuing the pregnancy involves a greater risk of injury to the physical or mental health of the existing members of the family,
(d) there is a substantial risk that the child will be born seriously deformed.

In 1977 the Parliamentary Committee which had been

appointed to scrutinise the operation of the 1967 Act concluded that there was no reason to amend the legislation:

We are unanimous in supporting the Act in its provisions. The passing of the Act exposed many personal problems in the lives of contemporary women which had previously been hidden and the inadequacy of the services which had been instituted to alleviate the problems. By facilitating a great number of abortions, the Act has relieved a vast amount of individual suffering. It has helped also to focus attention on the paramount need for preventative action, for more education in sex-life and its responsibilities and for the widespread provision of contraceptive advice and facilities. It has served to stimulate research into all aspects of abortion and the development of safer operative techniques. These have been undeniably great benefits. (The Abortion Act Inquiry: Lane Committee)

The Need for Choice

Were we to have abortion facilities under the provision of the 1967 Act in Northern Ireland, a woman here could make a free decision about what to do if she found herself with an unwanted pregnancy. This is the situation for which NIALRA is campaigning. Unlike the anti-abortion campaigns, we are not laying down a general rule of conduct for all women. We are not suggesting that abortion is the best or only solution to an unwanted pregnancy. We merely believe that women are the best judges of their own situation and that all choices, including that of abortion, should be available to them. The denial of the option of abortion is one more aspect of the restriction on women's lives in Northern Ireland. Women's lack of control over their bodies reflects a general lack of control over their lives.

Women do not make the decision to have an abortion lightly. No woman becomes pregnant in order to have an abortion. In Northern Ireland the number of women with unwanted pregnancies has much to do with the lack of childcare facilities and the inadequacy of sex education. Furthermore, it cannot be seen in isolation from the levels of poverty and unemployment. Yet it is noticeable that very few of those who are opposed to abortion are in the forefront of the struggle to remedy the conditions which frequently drive women to seek abortions. In Northern Ireland abortion is a class issue as well as a women's issue. Rich women have always been able to get abortion; poor women either cannot afford to go to England at all or do so with much difficulty and suffering, as the following example recounted by Naomi Wayne shows:

A couple of years ago I was passing through London and I stopped in at one of those private centres where they do abortions for women who come from abroad. There were two women from Northern Ireland. One was a young woman of twenty-one. This was a weekend. She worked in a shirt factory. She had left the factory at 4:30 on the Friday afternoon. She had travelled overnight. She had arrived in London on the Saturday. She had the abortion. She was travelling back to Northern Ireland on the Sunday so that she could be in work at eight o'clock without having lost a single second's wages. The reason that twenty-one year old woman was in London having an abortion and not in Liverpool having an abortion was because she was so badly paid that she had to keep working while pregnant in order to make enough money to pay for the abortion. And by the time that she had made enough money to pay for the abortion, her pregnancy was too advanced for the Liverpool clinic to do it; so, she had to go to London. She couldn't afford to take a second off work.

It has been argued that there is no need for abortion in Northern Ireland where contraception is available. The fact that contraception is technically freely available here belies the reality that access to it is restricted in a society such as ours which is permeated by repressive attitudes towards sexuality. The churches exhort us to beware of the 'contraceptive mentality'. The problem really is that we do not have a contraceptive mentality. Focusing on contraception, however, may reduce but not eradicate the numbers of women seeking abortions. There is still no safe and effective method of contraception. Improvement of access to contraception must accompany, not replace, the provision of legal abortion facilities.

An instance of the extreme hypocrisy of anti-abortion groups in Ireland - be they SPUC, LIFE the Churches or political parties - is that, while condemning women who seek abortions, they do little or nothing to remove, indeed they often reinforce, the stigma attached to unmarried mothers. The same groups profess to feel concern about the guilt women are said to feel after having had abortions. It is public statements and propaganda put forward by these groups which create the guilt and shame some women may endure and which drive them into positions of silence and isolation. Of the many thousands of Northern Ireland women who have had abortions, there are very few who can openly acknowledge their experience even to those closest to them.

The Demand for Abortion

The anti-abortion lobby argues that there is no demand for abortion in Northern Ireland. Furthermore, SPUC and LIFE claim that the majority of people here are against the extension of the 1967 Act. The fact is that public opinion here has never been properly tested. But, even if it was found that the majority of people are opposed to abortion, that would not be sufficient reason for failing to change the law. In England the 1967 Act was introduced without a majority of the people demanding it. It was a response to the most pressing demand of all - the demand of women seeking abortions. At the current rate, fifteen out of every one hundred women in Northern Ireland will have an abortion during their lives. That is the demand to which SPUC and LIFE have no answer. It is that demand which is the most compelling reason for extending the 1967 Act.

The European Dimension

Northern Ireland lags behind most other European countries in providing women with the option of abortion. On 10 February 1981 the European Parliament discussed the topic of abortion in the context of the position of women within member countries of the EEC. The Parliament called for the end of 'abortion tourism' within the member states:

The European Parliament ... notes that the relevant legislation in member states varies so widely that women in distress frequently have to seek help in other countries, and requests the Commission to press the Council for decisions at national level such as to obviate the need for journeys of this type which make any form of social aid impossible and lead to unacceptable commercialisation, and to ensure that every woman who finds herself in difficulty can obtain the necessary assistance in her own country. (The Position of Women in the European Community, European Parliamentary Debate, Luxembourg, June 1981)

The Benefits of Liberalisation

The experience of European countries which have legalised abortion has shown that the liberalisation of the law has had beneficial effects. Backstreet abortions and/or self-induced terminations with their often dangerous consequences have almost disappeared. It has enabled a more open discussion of previously taboo subjects such as contraception, sex education and sexuality in general.

After a country has legalised abortion there has usually been an immediate increase in the number of abortions carried out. This is only natural as those who previously would have had to have a backstreet abortion or to travel abroad are now being represented in the official figures. There might also be a slight increase in the actual number of abortions performed, because women might avail themselves of an option previously denied. This has been used by many anti-abortion campaigners as an argument against the extension of the 1967 Act to Northern Ireland. As international comparison shows, the argument is not valid. In fact, when seen in the long term, almost all countries which have legalised abortion have experienced a sharp decrease in abortion figures. The reason for this decline is related to the greater knowledge of and access to contraception and a more liberal climate of opinion which has accompanied the legalisation of abortion. It is this more conscious awareness of sexuality which we feel is needed in Northern Ireland to prevent unwanted pregnancies and therewith reduce the number of abortions necessary.

Northern Ireland Abortion Law Reform Association
1985

Across the Water

*We in the Irish Women's Abortion Support Group (IWASG),
wrote the following story as an illustration of how it is for an
Irish woman who has an unwanted pregnancy. The problems
that the woman faces are common to many Irish women but the
story is also one of the more heartening examples; because the
woman has access to information and some money, and she is
not alone in dealing with her termination. We decided not to
write it in an objective way, listing the various issues that
women face, as this would not necessarily provide a useful basis
for understanding the situation in which Irish women decide to
have an abortion and carry it out. We hope that writing in this
way, describing the circumstances which are fairly typical of
women who come here, will give some idea of the problems faced
by women in more difficult situations, particularly in the climate
of silence and repression that presently exists in Ireland. It is
clear that women in Ireland are not letting the political and
social situation get them down; they are finding ways to do what
they need to do. Often the difficult choice of an abortion is an
empowering one for women. They go back, not only with the will
to survive, but with a greater drive to fight back. The resilience
and strength of the individual women we meet is an ongoing
source of encouragement to us in IWASG.*

He wasn't your typical romantic, tall, dark and handsome,
with a chest of 42, but I kinda liked him. He was the one
that came with the bread in the morning just before we
opened up. And it came as no surprise to anyone when we
started going out together. He used to pick me up from the
shop on Friday night and we'd go up to de Barra's pub to
meet the lads.

There was always a gang of us up there and after a few
we'd go up to Hooley's disco. The thing I liked best about
him was that he'd dance the fast ones as well as the slow
and he wasn't afraid of making a fool of himself. He used
to pretend he was a mad passionate lover, dancing with

wild abandon to the fast ones and slow and smoochy to the others. Basically he was good for a laugh and I can't resist anyone with a sense of humour. We were always slagging each other (which in our gang meant that we liked each other), we had a good *craic* (fun) anyway.

Whenever we didn't get on, something would remind us of a funny thing one of us had said and we'd soon be laughing at it all. One night we both got kinda carried away - I mean, I always wanted to know what it would be like, so I suppose I let it happen. God, it was only the once. Wouldn't you know our family would be one of the most fertile! I come from a family of five, so you know yourself. Not being immediately clued-in to what was happening, I was six weeks before it dawned on me and anyway I didn't really want to admit it. There seemed no way of getting away from it but I had to find out for sure. I knew I could get a pregnancy test from the chemist's but I wasn't going to go into McCarthy's, was I, so I had to change my usual Saturday morning shift with Doreen and hitch a lift to Ballybrophy. It was fourteen miles away so I thought I'd be all right. Well, after plucking up the courage I got the kit and my worst fears were found out. Bloody hell, what was I going to do? I was twenty-three and hardly in the position to bring up a baby and anyway how could I tell my mother? She'd die. She had always trusted me and it would have felt like a betrayal - I couldn't do that to her. Anyway, I knew that if I told anyone I'd have no say about what would happen, so I didn't.

I felt a real criminal leaving the house that night shrouded in the secrecy of my abortion - how could I even think about it? The silence was choking me, but if I even gave a hint to my mother about what I was going to do I'd be out on my ear. My mother would not have been able to accept that I had sex, and to her mind 'killing a baby' would be tantamount to siding with the devil. The pregnancy alone would have been enough to banish me to some hostel in the city, to wait out the nine months in fear and self-loathing, to have to feel grateful for the patronising benevolence of the nuns who were kind enough to take me in. And to wait silently and without reproach, the time when I would have my child taken from me. I couldn't face all that. No, I couldn't live with the fear and the self-loathing so I chose to abort and whatever your morals I know it was the right decision for me.

I was the moodiest person you could meet then. One minute I'd be all cheerful and the next I'd be down in the dumps. I knew I'd have to tell someone, otherwise someone might guess and start to ask me what was wrong and I couldn't trust myself not to cry. I felt I had no real friends. I had plenty of acquaintances but no one to really talk to. Eileen was the only one. Her parents are very strict but she always takes the piss out of the way they over-react to things. Well, I did talk to her and I'll tell you one thing, you never know anyone well enough when it comes to telling them something difficult; you always end up blurting it out, taking a chance and hoping for the best. Eileen just stopped in her tracks, didn't move another step for a minute, then continued up the road to the post office, and I told her I was posting a letter to an abortion clinic in England (I had got their address in *Cosmo* and I wanted to know how much it would cost and all the details). Eileen said that a friend of hers in Cork had heard of a group in London that helps women like me, and she said she'd write to them and find out more about them.

'Course, I didn't know it at the time but the two clinics in Dublin, the Well Woman and Open Line, had been closed by a High Court ruling, so there was nowhere to find that kind of information.

Luckily for me though, a small group of women in Cork had decided that they were not going to stand for that and they defy the High Court ruling by distributing leaflets in Cork City at weekends, and by running a helpline. It was like a godsend when I found out about them, only 'god' isn't the right word really, is it? Anyway I rang them up and in a kinda roundabout way they managed to tell me about Imelda[1] in London, whom I should contact. The phone was a big problem for me. We're not on the automatic in Caherconnell and whenever I'd use the phone I'd have to be careful in case the operator would overhear.

Well, it just meant I'd have to make another trip to

Ballybrophy to phone London. The problem was how I was going to explain to my mother where I was going on a Tuesday evening, a work-night after all, and Mrs Kennedy wouldn't be pleased if I wasn't in the following morning at eight, to do the stocktaking. I just said I was going out to Margaret's. At that stage I didn't care how odd it looked. I just had to get to Ballybrophy that night and Imelda would only be on the line from six to nine.

While I was waiting for a lift I was thinking of the money I'd need. The clinic had written back to me with details. It would be almost £200 for the abortion itself and at least £50 for the trip and £20 or so for accommodation and God knows what else I'd need for the things that might happen on the way - Jesus, it was all too much. Lucky for me I was picked up by somebody from the other side of town and they didn't know me. I just said I was from Ballybrophy and that I had got held up visiting an aunt in the town. I had already decided I was going to tell the person on the way back the same story in reverse.

Anyway, I got through to Imelda, after about half an hour - the line's always busy. She seemed nice on the phone. She told me it would be a little cheaper than I thought (which was a great relief to me) and she said that she or one of her friends could put me up and that I shouldn't worry about the money and just come if I had made up my mind. I was eight weeks by then and it would take a while to get enough money together for the trip and also to arrange another Saturday off.

Eileen had been great all along. It was good to be able to talk to her about what I was doing. It was she who persuaded me to tell Eamonn. I had put it off, really. I just didn't want anybody to try and change my mind so I stopped seeing him. When I told him he was shocked. He didn't try to deny responsibility or anything. How could he anyway? Though I suppose he could have tried it on. Instead he said he'd stand by my decision - typical really 'cause he couldn't make up his own mind about anything and he didn't have any money that he could give towards the cost. He doesn't earn much more than me on £58 a week and he has to give most of it to his mother because his father isn't working. So I suppose he wasn't much help in a practical sense, but it brought us back together and we're a lot closer now. We're both sad that it happened but we know that it was the only thing we could do really, given the situation. We both want to have children in the future.

Anyway, I'm going off the point a bit. Eileen put me on the bus to Cork. I was supposed to be going to stay with her friend Breda. Only, once I arrived in Cork I hopped on the bus for London. After the consultation in the clinic, Imelda's friend Siobhán, another woman from IWASG, took me to her house. She couldn't have been nicer really. She didn't ask me too many questions, which was great 'cause I was a bit paranoid that it would get back to them at home. I was really glad she was Irish too; she just understood when I told her about the lies I had to tell to get to England and she just listened to what I had to say and didn't judge me. If I could do half as much for somebody else as she did for me, I'd be doing a lot.

Now that it's all over, Eileen and I are thinking of ways we could help other women. We'd like to be able to do what the women in Cork do, but leafleting is out of the question because we'd be kicked out of home if we started that and the phone of course is another no-go area because of the operator system. But at least a group of us now meet and talk amongst ourselves about how we can bring it up in conversations with other women we know.

Irish Women and Abortion - Some of the Facts

According to official statistics 5,642 Irish women, residents of the North and South of Ireland, had abortions in 1986. We assume that this is an underestimate because many women give English addresses as a form of disguise.

The women who come to England for terminations vary in age and class, and come from all over the country. One of the London clinics used by a large number of Irish women provides us with statistical information on a regular basis. This shows:

- The largest number of women who have terminations are between the ages of 20-25.
- The majority of women are single but the number of

married women is significant too, given the supposed sanctity of family life in Ireland.

- A large proportion of women come from Dublin but a surprising number of women from rural Ireland make their way to England. It is especially difficult for women who live outside cities to get the information they need and to make telephone calls, and travelling to England can be a complicated business.
- In recent years more working-class and poor women are deciding to have abortions. This is a change as previously it was mainly middle-class and professional women who pursued this option.
- What is most surprising is that a very high proportion of women's gestation periods are twelve weeks and under. Given the difficulties involved in getting to England - finance, information, travel - it is a major feat that so many women can make it within the first twelve weeks. However, the Alton Bill will affect Irish women: in 1986 5.25 per cent of Irish women had abortions after eighteen weeks and this proportion increased during 1987 (complete figures are not yet available). This compares with 3.11 per cent of women resident in England and Wales.

The IWASG - Who We Are

IWASG is an Irish women's collective based in London. It has been in existence since 1981. Over the years we've thought about opening the group to women who are not Irish but we've decided against doing this for political and practical reasons. The group is a positive strengthening experience for us, although we also have our differences. We work closely with other women who are interested in the issues and who are willing to provide the support we need. We are based at the Women's Reproductive Rights Information Centre, which is a significant source of encouragement and support. We have for many years worked in close co-operation with the Spanish Women's Abortion Support Group. Anti-Irish racism is still rampant in this country. In the course of our work we constantly encounter views that Irish people are stupid and particularly backward around issues related to sexuality.

While the national government in the South is undoubtedly reactionary in its approach to reproductive rights, it hardly represents the views or aspirations of the entire population of Ireland. It is clear from our experience that women are often intimidated by being in London: it is a strange city, people speak a different language - English it may be, but it is different; their reason for being here is often fraught with tension. In the circumstances it is hardly surprising that women feel out of control and are often very sensitive to anti-Irish comments. We work from the basis that we have a shared past, that we understand where women are coming from, the values they hold, what they feel about being here and that we are equipped to provide the support, particularly the emotional support, that women may need.

Women choose to get involved in IWASG for different reasons. For some it provides the opportunity to continue their involvement in issues that they'd previously worked on in Ireland. For others of us it is a practical way of taking some action around an important issue. We are conditioned as women to be helpful, to look after other people, but there seems to be a contradiction in providing support for women having abortions, as it would never be seen to be a good cause by either our families or the Irish state. It is a subversive activity: enabling women to have terminations undermines the dominant values of both the Church and State in Ireland. The work also provides the opportunity to have active political connections with Ireland through liaising with groups who are also active around similar issues there. Our ongoing contact with women who come over for abortions keeps us aware of what is happening in women's lives in Ireland. Through them we are also reminded of the culture we left behind, ways of expressing ourselves, gestures and ways of seeing the world which we sometimes forget as we are absorbed into living here. Many of us in the group do not tell our families about our involvement in IWASG. It is a well-guarded secret, something we often share with the women coming over, many of whom cannot tell family or friends why they are coming here.

The Work of IWASG

We approach the issues raised by the situation in Ireland in relation to abortion in different ways. (Not only is abortion illegal in Ireland, in the South it is also illegal to provide information which would enable women to get abortions.)

The service aspect of the work is the most time-consuming. It includes running a phone line to Ireland one night each week (we are planning to increase this to two evenings). Women (and occasionally men) call us to find out information about the services over here, to book terminations and to talk about what is happening in their lives. We organise women's appointments at the clinics, which often includes negotiating financial deals with the clinics, as many women do not have the ready cash needed for what is now an expensive trip to London. For some women it is their first trip to London, and often their first time out of Ireland. We arrange to meet them at their points of arrival when we have the resources to do this. Women are required by law to spend the night before the operation in England, which means that they have to be accommodated overnight. We use a combination of bed-and-breakfast accommodation and our own homes, depending on how much money women can afford to spend and our own resources for putting people up. We have on a few occasions also looked after children while their mothers were staying overnight in the clinic, which reflects how desperate women's situations are and their lack of support at home.

Supporting the women who come for abortions is the core of our work. It makes large demands on our time, energy and emotions, and requires an imaginative approach to planning. What happens if you have two women staying, one has a miscarriage in the night and the other doesn't feel confident enough to find her way to the clinic the next morning? This has happened. Women sometimes phone from pay phones as soon as they've arrived. They don't know what to do, where to go. To date, we've managed to respond to all the calls we've had. On the basis of a telephone call, or two, we assess how much support women need and attempt to give it. With some women we only have telephone contact, organising their appointments, their accommodation and maybe phoning them during their stay at the clinic. We also support each other, by being available to discuss the difficulties that arise so that no woman is left on her own to sort out a situation that turns out to be more problematic than anticipated.

Before the abortion referendum [1983] in Ireland we dealt only with emergencies, that is, we helped women who found it difficult to cope with being here, or who needed financial support. They were mostly referred through the counselling services in Dublin or by other agencies. Since the closure of these services, our work has expanded to include arranging abortions.

We liaise with those groups who are active around abortion issues in Ireland, both in the North and South, including those groups which run phone lines and abortion campaign groups. Through them we keep in touch with what happens in Ireland at a political and policy level. We collaborate on publicity and in our use of the Press, we provide speakers for events in Ireland, and they send speakers to events here. This link is crucial as it provides the dynamic which gives the service its political direction.

Publicity is an important dimension of the group's work. Part of our role is educational, providing information about what is happening in Ireland around reproductive rights, or the lack of them. Most of our success in raising issues is done in co-operation with the left and the women's press. While it is important and useful to raise issues in these areas, we do want to have access to a wider audience. Gaining access to the national media is very difficult. For the most part it is not interested in the everyday issues and we sometimes feel misrepresented. It has also been our intention for some time now to gain access to the Irish media. This is not easy either. The Irish press based here ignores us and has refused to publish our publicity material. Our work is not visible in the larger Irish community here. It is therefore our intention to inform Irish people living here beyond our own network of the extent to which Irish women are seeking terminations, and the issues that raises for them.

IWASG is unfunded. We've never been eligible for public funding as the service offered is for women who are not resident in this country. We have no paid workers. Women commit as much or as little time as they can according to their various other commitments. Fundraising is an ongoing nightmare but it can sometimes be fun too. We pursue the usual array of fundraising activities - letters to charities, begging letters to the rich amongst us, sponsored swims, walks and benefits. The money raised is used to subsidise women who cannot afford to pay for their abortions. This is an ever-increasing number as more and more working-class and poor women decide to have terminations. It is not possible to use the National Health Service; women are therefore always in the position of having to pay, apart from the small number of free beds we manage to negotiate from the clinics.

Given our ongoing need for money we would appreciate a donation, however small. Our address [1992] is: IWASG, c/o 52-54 Featherstone Street, London EC1Y 8RT.

Irish Women's Abortion Support Group
1988

Note
1 'Imelda' was a code name for the Irish Women's Abortion Support Group.

Abortion: Myths and Realities from the Irish Folk Tradition

There are many myths and many realities concerning the practice of abortion in Ireland. In this article I wish to explore those myths and realities as revealed by Irish folklore and popular culture. It is the social and historical construction of an ideology of womanhood and motherhood, in the Irish experience, which will be examined. Contemporary folklore in Ireland, and the current debate about abortion or related practices, will be regarded in the light of the Irish folk tradition and its heritage to contemporary Irish society.

Introduction

What is the Irish folk tradition, and how can it elucidate myths and realities about abortion in Ireland? Folk culture is an unwritten, traditional body of knowledge and experience, passed on from one individual, group or generation to another. It is dynamic, and it is an honest reflection of prevalent concerns, mores and prejudices within communities and cultures. Irish folklore has been systematically collected in this country since the foundation of the Irish Folklore Commission in 1935 (later becoming the Department of Irish Folklore at University College Dublin). The collecting of Irish oral traditions was pursued by a variety of individuals and groups, most notably in the early years, by Irish language enthusiasts and those with an antiquarian interest. The late nineteenth century growth of interest in collecting European folklore was part of the ethnocentric tracing of one's Aryan roots: a fact that situates the Grimm brothers, among others, in their social and historical context. This pan-European nationalist movement affected Ireland also. The search for, and collecting of, wonder-tales (a genre of the folktale, commonly called 'fairy stories') and the unearthing of lost cultures on the forgotten fringes of the European mainland, such as the western extremities of the islands of

Ireland or Scotland, was centred on this urge towards re-discovering and reclaiming Europe's lost soul. As part of that process, a body of information concerning social behaviour and habits, beliefs and customs was also collected by those cultural pioneers, thus augmenting knowledge of what was then deemed 'peasant cultures'. The 'noble savage' was alive and well and living, for example, on the Blasket Islands.

This is by way of introduction, for the topics of women's sexuality, childbirth or abortion were not prominent in this body of folklore, except insofar as they occurred in storytelling or in oral poetry. It is only relatively recently that these topics have been studied in themselves by Irish folklorists. Some material relating to these subjects was collected through the years by the Irish Folklore Commission and the Department of Irish Folklore at UCD. The full-time collector Michael J. Murphy was particularly interested in the collecting of folklore concerning sex and sexuality. In 1979 I circulated my first questionnaire, concerning 'Unbaptised Children' and then in 1983 the 'Childbirth' questionnaire, through the Department of Irish Folklore, as an aid in my research into the topics of sexuality and childbirth. Through the 1980s and 1990s these topics have received more and more attention. The supremacy of storytelling or *scealaíocht* has gradually been superseded by that of lore or *seanchas*. The analysis of this body of folkloric information provides fascinating insights into details of human life in Ireland, from both urban and rural areas, over the last one hundred years. And because it is folk tradition, this information hints at beliefs and customs which have survived in this country for hundreds of years. In this article, I will summarise from the existing material, to provide an overview of the sort of information available for analysis.

Penitentials

To situate briefly Ireland's Christian inheritance, the earliest recorded religious tracts which deal with the subject of abortion are the 'Penitentials'. From the second half of the sixth century, religious works, commonly called 'Penitentials', because they were manuals of private penance designed to assist the priest or spiritual guide by describing various types of sins and specifying appropriate penances, spread from Ireland, England and Wales throughout Europe (O'Connor 1991b). In the seventh century Irish Penitential of St Finnian, we read:

If a woman by her magic destroys the child she has conceived of somebody, she shall do penance for half a year with an allowance of bread and water, and abstain for two years from wine and meat and fast for the six forty-day periods with bread and water (Bieler, 1963).

Four other Irish penitential texts contain similar references (O'Connor 1991b). The Penitentials are one of the earliest available sources concerning Christian regulations regarding the practices of abortion, infanticide and child-abandonment. All of these practices were, of course, known in the pre-Christian world. Also, it is worth remembering that Christianity was introduced into different countries in Europe at different times: in parts of Scandinavia this was as late as the tenth and eleventh centuries. There is evidence in the Penitentials which indicates that the practices of abortion, the overlaying or smothering of newborn babies, and child abandonment, were well-known and legislated for by the early Christian Church. Complex regulations, for instance, relate to whether or not it was a poor woman who caused the child to die, in which case the punishment was considerably less. Forty days of pregnancy was the period taken as a boundary between whether or not the woman was seen as a murderess.

This is cited by way of background, and not least because there is a prevalent opinion that abortion was always considered a heinous crime in Christian terms. Through later historical periods, the analysis of how attitudes might have changed towards the taking of the life of an unborn child (or a newly-born baby) would require a detailed study for each particular period. For the purposes of this article, I wish to merely allude to the religious historical heritage on this subject. Space does not permit me to trace the development of thought, focusing on aspects of the medieval period, or the witchcraft trials, or the radical changes of the nineteenth century in terms of religious and sexual mores (O'Connor 1991b). Suffice to say that from the seventeenth century onwards there was a growing concern with the prevalence of 'illegitimacy', infanticide and abortion. All of which have had an influence in forming contemporary attitudes and beliefs.

Midwives

The realm of sexuality and childbirth has traditionally been perceived as that where women predominate. The midwife is the central figure in this domain. In Irish folklore, the midwife or handywoman, *bean chabhartha*, emerges as a woman of power: in tradition, these women were not only responsible for bringing new life into the world but they were also responsible for laying out the dead. This dual role, involving both the beginning and the end of life, was perceived as wielding power over life and death. It is not surprising, therefore, that the figure of the midwife is so prevalent in Irish, and European, folk belief and legend.

There is a richness of material concerning such figures as Biddy Early, for instance, in Irish folklore, who was believed to have special healing powers and the gift of clairvoyance. Biddy Early is not unusual: women accredited with similar powers were known and spoken about throughout the Irish countryside, and in the urban areas. Such 'wise women', *mná feasa*, and their male counterparts, *fir feasa*, were respected and feared. Theirs was the realm of white magic, witchcraft and the working of charms and spells. This is the *maleficia* which received such attack during the centuries of the witch-craze in Europe. Midwives, handywomen and herbalists of all types were included in this grouping of personages to whom supernatural powers were accredited. Some of these people were believed to have contact with the Otherworld, and to be invested with such Otherworld powers. In Irish traditional terms, otherworldly powers or supernatural agency not only comprised good and evil, but a twilight area of the neutral was also accommodated! Thus magic or supernatural power could be good or evil, depending on who used that power and for what purpose. The juxtaposition of good and evil, God and the Devil, was thus enhanced or complicated by neutral forces, which in Irish folklore, are those credited to the fairies, or 'good people'. In a tradition where 'God is good', 'the Devil isn't bad either', and 'the Devil looks after his own', it should not be so surprising to people in the 1990s to know that a lively faith in the fairies thrived amongst our foreparents. The evidence of this massive faith, which complemented and was accommodated by, the Roman Catholic Church and its faithful in this country, is contained in the Irish Folklore Collections, in innumerable writings on the subject, in our literature, music and folk song, and in the people around us.

Regarding the midwife, one of the most famous folk legends known in this country and throughout Europe, is the 'Midwife to the Fairies', classified as an international legend (Christiansen, 1958) concerning a midwife called to assist at a fairy-birth, with dramatic consequences for the woman.

It is important to note here, that, in historical terms, midwives throughout Europe were systematically marginalised in obstetrics and gynaecology since the Middle Ages, so that women practitioners became embroiled in:

a web of medical regulations and municipal ordinances aimed at either prohibiting their practice altogether or at least placing them under total control (Blumenfeld-Kosinski, 1990)

This is what Jo Murphy-Lawless has termed the 'colonisation of childbirth' (Murphy-Lawless 1988, 1991): an inevitable consequence of the professionalisation of medicine and the concomitant exclusion of women. Women were the primary victims of the witch hunts throughout Europe, and the figure of the witch-midwife was constructed in order to equate midwifery and satanism in the popular imagination (Blumenfeld-Kosinski, 1990; O'Connor 1988, 1991a, 1991b). The witch-midwife, as described in the *Malleus Maleficarum* (1486), written by two Dominican priests, Heinrich Kramer and Jakob Sprenger, is featured in such sections as 'That Women who are Midwives in Various Ways Kill the Child Conceived in the Womb, and Procure an Abortion; or if they do not this, Offer Newborn Children to Devils', or 'How Witch-Midwives commit most horrid Crimes when they either Kill Children or offer them to Devils in most Accursed Wise'. This book was published thirteen times in Europe by 1520; it was issued sixteen times in Germany and eleven times in France before 1700, and while it may have been in use in England, no English translation appeared in print until the nineteenth century (O'Connor, 1991b). The history of witch-hunting in Europe is extremely complex. In Ireland, there is little evidence of witch-trials or the witch-craze as the phenomenon is represented throughout the European mainland or in the New World. Magic, however, and its relationship with Otherworld powers was well-known in this country.

Abortion

Unwanted pregnancy, whether due to rape and sexual violence, or because of a fear of ostracisation and the stigma of illegitimacy, or because of a myriad of economic, social, personal or psychological reasons, has always constituted a dilemma for women. Innumerable methods said to be efficacious in causing abortions, have existed and have been recorded. From my analysis of Irish folklore sources, there is evidence that all manner of methods have been attempted, often resulting in the death of the mother as well as the death of the unborn child.

Efforts to induce abortion by external means, such as beatings, vigorous physical exertions (jumping over ditches, jumping down from tables and sheds, running large distances, carrying heavy loads etc), as well as the use of assorted instruments (iron hooks, coat-hangers etc) have all been recorded in Ireland. Similarly, a vast array of herbal concoctions (including rue, fennel, garlic etc), oral abortifacients and drugs have been named, such as: swallowing a mixture of saltpetre and a laxative, mixtures of various herbs, Epsom salts, quantities of gin and/or quinine, castor oil, Jeyes' Fluid or similar disinfectants, eating fine coal slack, brewing copper pennies and drinking the water in which they boiled, and mixing urine, onion and boiling water together in a basin, so that the woman could sit over the mixture and inhale it while keeping her feet in the mixture. Each of these 'solutions' finds ready parallel in the popular cultures of the rest of the world. In more recent urban folklore collecting in this country, some references to backstreet abortionists appear, such as the famous Nurse Cadden case in Dublin. From the folklore evidence, however, inducing 'natural' abortion seems to have been the preferred method: there is comparatively scant information available relating to the activities of 'professional' abortionists.

It must be remembered that midwives were indeed strictly controlled in this country, as elsewhere. The trend which started in the later Middle Ages continued and flourished, so that by the later nineteenth and early twentieth centuries, a large distinction was observed between those women who had professionally trained as midwives and those who learned their trade within the local community, the 'handywomen' and 'wise women'. This is an extremely important distinction, and one which is borne out by the evidence available to us in Irish folklore. Many of the women who contributed information to me, who were professional midwives, were very clear in pointing out that if any complications arose during a delivery they would immediately seek the assistance of a qualified doctor. Equally, none of those women ever said that they had assisted in providing an abortion for a woman. Midwives were forbidden to engage in any of the folk practices concerning abortion, as outlined above; handywomen, or any other women, however, were not influenced by official restrictions. Popular wisdom, as in all aspects of folk medicine, often intervened. If a woman was sufficiently desperate, she would presumably have resorted to whatever means of assistance presented themselves.

Popular Attitudes
Space does not permit an historical analysis of abortion in this country, or the detailed examination of Church and State directives on the subject. It is a complex social and historical situation. My aim is rather to indicate some of the insights to be gleaned from an examination of abortion in Irish folklore. The themes of abortion and infanticide, as

63

expressed in Irish folk belief and legend surrounding child murderess traditions, constitute another aspect of this discussion (O'Connor 1991b). In my detailed analysis of traditions of child murder in this country I concluded that popular beliefs and customs have been predominantly affected by Christian morals and teachings. This means that the traditions are profoundly religious in character, but that the popular attitudes encapsulated show, on the one hand, a rejection of a witch-midwife, unrepentant child murderess figure, and on the other, a sympathy with a Mary Magdalene, sinner-saint figure. Arguably, both bear witness to Christian thinking.

The witch-midwife, child murderess character could be either the mother of the unwanted child or a woman hired for the purpose of doing away with an unwanted child. In nearly all cases of the folk legend, infanticide, and not abortion, is the method of achieving this end. By contrast, abortion features in the folk ballad known as 'The Cruel Mother', versions of which have been collected in this country. The children's version is well-known under the title of 'Weela Weela Walia' (O'Connor 1991b).

In examining the corpus of material directly relating to abortion, and to midwives as traditionally dominant figures in the Irish folklore of childbirth, the popular attitudes expressed in folk belief and custom are predominantly practical. The fact of unwanted pregnancy is not ignored: stratagems of overcoming such an unwelcome situation are discussed, stories are told and songs are sung, and passed on from one person, group and generation to another. The dilemma which is the focus of the folklore material relating to infanticide, and which by extension, must also be related to abortion, is that children who are not baptised are not afforded the same joys in the afterlife as those who are baptised, according to Roman Catholic teaching. This lack of baptism was central in the traditional community, in influencing attitudes towards the topics of abortion and infanticide. By comparison with contemporary concerns, this is significantly lacking. The present discourse on the right to life of the unborn child has never adequately addressed the issue of whether or not unbaptised children (including thereby aborted foetuses) are granted the Beatific Vision in the Otherworld, or whether they are relegated to the twilight zone of Limbo. This fear was a motivating factor in the lives of our foreparents. The fear of divine retribution for committing sin, and the agony for women who had to have abortions even though they knew they were thereby depriving their child of eternal life has been well documented. Many references to women trying to baptise the child or foetus in their womb, before having an abortion, exist.

Conclusion

The Irish folk heritage with regard to abortion is a complex one, therefore, reflecting as it does the complexities of life, the impossible decisions and choices forced upon people, and the consequences of making those choices. What is most heartening in examining the Irish folk material on sexuality and childbirth is that there is always a balance of opinions, just like the neutral concepts discussed above; while 'right' and 'wrong' exist, nevertheless the realm of the in-between, the not-so-clear, trusting in the greater wisdom or understanding of God (or humanity) in judging individuals for their individual choices and actions is affirmed. The moral of 'let he who has no sin amongst you cast the first stone' seems to have been important for our foreparents. Learning from the wealth of our folklore heritage, and distinguishing the myths and realities in the popular history of abortion in this country, might assist in bringing some mature and non-judgemental, practical wisdom to the current debates about abortion in Ireland.

Anne O'Connor
1992

The Obstetric View of Feminine Identity
A Nineteenth Century Case History of the Use of Forceps on Unmarried Women in Ireland

Obstetric Discourses and the Issue of Control

With increasing conflict between women and obstetricians about how birth is managed, during the very recent past feminists have challenged the obstetric view that childbirth must be a medical event.[1] The feminist critique of current obstetric practice points out that at the core of the debate is the issue of who controls women in birth, and feminists have demanded both an end to unnecessary medical intervention and a return to women-centred and women-controlled reproductive care.[2]

However, in positing a 'golden age' of women-controlled childbirth which we must now try and regain (Macintyre, 1977), the feminist argument fails to examine the nature and extent of obstetric power. In speaking simply of male takeover from women, the argument fails to examine the crucial role obstetric discourse played in achieving male control over women giving birth. Using discourse, obstetric science created an ideology about labouring women which was then imposed through clinical practice. While necessarily contesting the ideology which makes up the obstetric view of women, the feminist critique has paid insufficient attention to the importance of obstetric discourses as the source of that ideology. It has not examined how these discourses were able to link ideology and practice and what the resulting impact was on women's identities as childbearers. The ideology of male-controlled childbirth and its effects on women in labour warrant detailed analysis. I want to explore this area, using a series of clinical reports compiled during the 1870s, at the internationally renowned Rotunda Hospital in Dublin, in which the use of forceps, particularly on unmarried women, was advocated as an acceptable clinical practice. This incident of the 1870s exemplifies what the ideology of male-controlled childbirth made possible.

The establishment of male-controlled childbirth

throughout Europe and the United States during the eighteenth century involved far more than the ousting of women midwives from their traditional role as birth attendants. In constructing a science of childbirth to secure their professional ambitions, men midwives invented a new object of attention in their discourses, that of the poor suffering women in labour. As a result women experienced a radical break in the social practices surrounding childbirth. The new science gave rise to the institution of the lying-in hospital. Crucial to the way that lying-in hospitals were to function, and to the power that men midwives came to exercise over women in labour, were their discourses on childbirth.

Over a period of more than 200 years these medical discourses have argued that women, by their very nature, are incapable of negotiating the hazards of childbirth both as reproducers and as managers, and thus require male intervention and control.

During the eighteenth century, men midwives, as they called themselves, advanced new theories about women in childbirth, based on an account of female sexuality which declared that women had certain essential or basic qualities. This 'essentialist' account, also reflected in the philosophical works of the period, maintained that women were endowed with a complex of physical characteristics, principally the softness and feebleness of their reproductive organs from which their psychological traits of dependence and passivity developed (Bloch and Bloch, 1980; Jordanova, 1980; Easlea, 1981; McLaren, 1984). These qualities of softness and dependence were seen as the essence of female nature. It was this essential female nature which rendered women physically and emotionally incompetent to undergo labour. Rather than defining female reproductive organs as being pliable and elastic, men midwives interpreted a woman's 'soft parts' as muscular feebleness. Using the sexual metaphor of the conquest and penetration of female nature common to the scientific discourses of the period, men midwives spoke of the (male) foetus in its descent of the birth canal as acting like a battering ram against woman's 'soft parts'.[3]

Childbirth was then defined as an overwhelmingly dangerous and painful natural practice which, given the inherent weakness of women, threatened their lives. Thus Fielding Ould, an eminent Irish man midwife wrote: 'In the most favourable labours poor women endure as much pain as mortals are well able to undergo' (Ould, 1742). Another Irish man midwife, Frederick Jebb, in describing the course of labour, said:

We cannot sufficiently admire the intention of Providence in thus ordering the matter ... in the period between the pains, the woman is perfectly in repose ... were the whole labour one continual state of pain, how few would live to see the end of it. And amongst the few that might possibly outlive the operation, I believe scarcely one would recover from the enfeebled state which such horror must reduce the strongest constitution. (Jebb, 1770)

In his *Treatise of Midwifery*, Ould insisted that 'the course of pain and danger which women undergo from the time of pregnancy till some time after birth is very considerable' (1742), on which he based his conclusions that the proper course of action for the man midwife was to 'hasten labour' and 'lessen pain'. By developing these premises about women's natural physical incapacity to deal with labour, the medical discourses in the eighteenth century turned childbirth into a continuing event which then required the scientific practice of the men midwives to see it through to a successful conclusion. With their invention of 'the poor suffering woman' as Ould always referred to women in labour, men midwives raised the argument about the pain and danger of labour to the status of a scientific truth, and the conceptual framework about women shaped the evolution of the science of childbirth.

There were strong links between the new science of childbirth and political practices which enabled the setting up of lying-in hospitals. The construction of the female body in labour as a problem was connected with the economic function of birth, a theme pursued in the general philosophical and economic discourses of the period. Classic mercantalist arguments which concentrated on the political mathematics of the population issue weighed reproductive outcomes in economic terms and contributed to the interest in childbirth and in the management of women as childbearers. The medical discourses which designated the female body as an important source of scientific inquiry mirrored the growing awareness of the body's potential as the ultimate source from which time and labour could be extracted.

Men midwives made constant reference to their role in preserving the 'life of the species'. Fielding Ould, for instance, wrote that midwifery was not 'the meanest province in the medicinal Commonwealth, but much on the contrary, as on it depends not only the preservation of the species but the various methods of relieving distressed women from extraordinary pain and torture, innumerable disorders and death ... ' (Ould, 1742). In this context, lying-in hospitals were seen as life-preserving institutions for women. According to Bartholomew Mosse, the man midwife credited with founding the Rotunda Hospital in Dublin, it offered shelter and skilled care to women otherwise 'destitute of attendance, medicine and often proper food, by which hundreds perish with their little infants and the community is at once robbed of both mother and child' (Browne, 1947). However, lying-in hospitals also provided the setting where theories about women and childbirth could be practiced on a specific population. The power of men midwives to control women in childbirth lay in their ability to postulate a connection between the individual body and the needs of the social body.[4]

The Contradictory Effects of Bio-Politics
The Rotunda Lying-in Hospital, begun in 1745, was the first lying-in hospital in the British Isles. At that time, the contemporary perception that poverty was far greater in Ireland than elsewhere in the British Isles provoked great concern about the country's economic development. In the documentation which supported the Rotunda's establishment, the relief of poor lying-in women was seen to have a strategic function. Mercantalist opinion held that greater numbers of manual and agricultural workers would increase national wealth. If the Rotunda took on the task of overseeing the labours of women from the working

classes, it would contribute to the national economy because 'the increase of inhabitants most to be desired is amongst the lowest ranks'.[5]

The 'poor suffering' women in labour of the men midwives' discourses were thus conflated with the 'labouring poor' and the lying-in hospital was regarded as a new form of charity. As Ould remarked in his *Treatise*, 'the poor who are by much the greater number (are) most subject to misfortunes in childbearing' (Ould, 1792). The social fact of poverty was added to the argument about women's natural incapacity to justify the existence of a lying-in hospital to monitor childbirth. The poor also provided a continuing source of clinical material, an advantage to themselves of which the men midwives were well aware.[6]

Clinical records were kept from 1786 onwards. Up to then, the hospital registry had noted the number of women admitted and the number of children born alive, that is, information related to how many people the hospital assisted as a charity. With the inception of clinical records, the emphasis shifted from statistics on poor labouring women to the process of labour itself. The records can be seen as chronicles of how men midwives objectified a woman in labour. She was fragmented into symptoms, cases, and complications. By the middle of the nineteenth century, even though the Rotunda was still a charitable institution, the detailed clinical records were evidence of the hospital's primary function as a medical establishment.

When Sinclair and Johnston, two assistant masters of the Rotunda, published their *Practical Midwifery* in 1858, the text exemplified the clinical approach. They proffered the obstetric outcomes of 13,748 cases as proof of the success of the Rotunda's approach to childbirth management. Sinclair and Johnston wrote in detail about the surveillance that had evolved around women in labour so that dress, diet, management of the stages of labour, position for birth, length of bedrest, and the timing of discharge were all standardised norms imposed on women at the hospital's discretion. Obstetric management decreeing how women should labour and for how long was the crucial layer of authority over the 'fit objects of charity' because it had the power to direct women's bodies in labour in accordance with the perceptions of men midwives.

In the main, Sinclair and Johnston used maternal mortality statistics to make their point about the Rotunda having a superior system in comparison to other lying-in hospitals. They collated their figures so as to present the most optimistic profile. The earliest clinical records had distinguished between maternal deaths related to the 'efforts of nature' and deaths from the 'efforts of art' that is, interventions by men midwives. Sinclair and Johnston in an equally arbitrary but more politic use of categories divided deaths into three categories: the first those deaths from 'accidents' of puerperal fever, which they claimed were beyond their control. Puerperal fever was the dangerous, life-threatening infection which could set in after a woman had given birth. In the second category they included all other deaths which did not arise from the 'effects of labour,' according to them, and finally in the third category were deaths which they thought did arise from the 'effects of labour.'

The aim was to have as few cases as possible in the third category, on which men midwives rested their reputation. Sinclair and Johnston listed the 163 deaths out of 13,748 cases as being in the proportion of one in 84/1/3. Subtracting those who died of puerperal fever, death being 'accidental,' the proportion of maternal deaths from all the other cases was shifted to read one in 148/3/4. Again subtracting deaths men midwives attributed to women's general weakness, unrelated to the 'effects of labour,' Sinclair and Johnston arrived at the 'true' rate of maternal mortality, those deaths which were calculated to have resulted from labour, as being one in 295/2/5 proportionately of the 13,748 women delivered. The labouring woman had been turned into a process and reduced to a fraction.

This play with numbers and categories of maternal deaths was a significant discourse of the period. Lying-in hospitals were alert to the need to secure their reputations professionally and politically, and the maternal mortality rates were a highly sensitive indicator on both counts. Assertions about successful systems of childbirth management were based on these statistics; the lower the rate that could be recorded, the better proof of superior management. These figures came to dominate medical journals in the nineteenth century as men midwives throughout the British Isles expounded their theories and techniques in competition with one another, each using his connection with a lying-in hospital as the source of his clinical material.

A higher rate of maternal mortality also had immediate political repercussions, particularly when an increase was traced to puerperal fever. For though Sinclair and Johnston tried to classify it as an accident, puerperal fever was firmly identified by the nineteenth century with lying-in hospitals.[7] In the period before sepsis and anti-sepsis were understood, and before the advent of antibiotics, what was clear to men midwives was that puerperal fever flourished in the hospital setting, an unintended consequence of the institutionalisation of childbirth. Because women could be affected by an outbreak, the fever had a disastrous impact and the only method of containing it was to close down wards where it occurred.

Puerperal fever undermined the rationale of lying-in hospitals to preserve the lives of poor women as reproducers. The funding of the hospitals, either by benefaction or by the state, was dependent on the success which they were seen to have in achieving their aim. Too high a number of maternal deaths led to public concern. The Rotunda itself faced closure four times in the nineteenth century because of puerperal fever epidemics. Yet even when both hospital and public authorities were sufficiently alarmed as to post notices around the city asking women to remain at home to give birth, destitute women were still presenting themselves at the door of the hospital seeking shelter where they could give birth.

The existence of puerperal fever exposed men midwives to the negative aspects of the breadth of clinical material they otherwise enjoyed. Firstly, they were confronted with the failure of their science. They could name the fever, dissect its victims, describe it, but in no way control it. Yet they and their hospitals seemed to set it in motion. Secondly, the women who came to the Rotunda were highly susceptible. They often suffered from the cumulative effect of poverty and malnutrition. Some had travelled a great distance, arriving at the Rotunda in an exhausted condition, sometimes already in labour. They were ill-equipped to deal with the consequences of an infection which ran rife in the hospital with contamination spread by men midwives.

Originally in setting up the Rotunda, men midwives had claimed a dual authority over the lives of women, first as arbiters of a charity whose function was to regulate and preserve the lives of the poor, and also as practitioners whose control of the female body in labour was the basis for the definitive science of obstetrics they were constructing. These two roles were increasingly thwarted because of the unexplained prevalence of puerperal fever. The Rotunda's status as an asylum for women seemed to men midwives a growing threat to its status as a scientific establishment. Puerperal fever was perceived by them as a malady afflicting poor women in the main and only occasionally affecting middle-class and upper-class women whom men midwives assisted in giving birth at home.[8]

In seeking to resolve the problems set in motion by the fever, the medical authorities in the Rotunda sought an answer at the expense of the women coming to the hospital. Men midwives had always contended that labour was complicated by the physical and psychological incompetence of women. They now extended this explanation to a hypothesis about puerperal fever. The fever seemed to be most prevalent among women carrying illegitimate babies. It was claimed that the disturbed psychological state of women encouraged the fever to take root. In this way, men midwives concocted an answer to the charge that they fostered puerperal fever: women were forced to bear the responsibility both for their marginalised social status and for their deaths in childbirth.[9]

Puerperal Fever, Seduction, and the Usefulness of Forceps

Sinclair and Johnston's attempt to present the lowest possible maternal mortality figures by disclaiming responsibility for deaths from puerperal fever did not stem the growing public disquiet about the issue. From 1851 to 1861, the number of admissions to the Rotunda fell by almost a quarter while the rate of maternal mortality increased to 2.4 per cent of annual admissions (by comparison with the maternal mortality rate for 1829-59 of 1.34 per cent). Puerperal fever was rampant and a further investigation by the Public Health Commissioners in 1856 ended with a recommendation that the Rotunda establish immediately an external department from which men midwives would go out and supervise births for women in their homes, thus reducing the numbers of hospital admissions. In 1863, the hospital closed with another epidemic.

In 1867, a former master, Evory Kennedy wrote to the board of governors at the Rotunda quoting figures on the large drop in admissions. Acknowledging competition from other lying-in hospitals, he nevertheless attributed the drop principally to the public fear about puerperal fever:

Puerperal fever ... is known to haunt our lying-in hospitals as its peculiar habitat, and so great are its ravages ... and such the proportion of victims swept away by it ... that there are physicians and philantropists who even question whether lying-in hospitals, as generally constructed, do not prove rather a curse than a blessing to the lying-in patient. (Kennedy, 1867)

The ravages of the fever had given rise to the now 'prevalent idea of recoveries being better at their own homes than in hospital', said Kennedy, which notion accounted for the drop in admissions. To preserve the opportunities for midwifery practice, Kennedy suggested that the main body of the hospital no longer be used for lying-in women, that a series of chalets be built to one side which could accommodate some women and that the external department be extended so that many more women could be dealt with at home. The main building could be used to extend the teaching facility of the hospital, concentrating on gynaecological practice so that the Rotunda as the location for a 'school of instruction' need not be abandoned.

The hospital governors rejected Kennedy's proposals but he returned to his criticism of the large hospital system which he saw as responsible for puerperal fever, with a paper delivered to the Dublin Obstetrical Society in 1869. Kennedy was not the first to point out that puerperal fever seemed less of a problem in small cottage hospitals in Ireland. But as a former master of the Rotunda, Kennedy aroused a great deal of anger amongst men midwives attached to the Rotunda. The ensuing discussions about his views amounted to more than 200 pages in the Society's journal. Kennedy was universally derided by his colleagues for his views which were taken as an attack on the scientific ethos of obstetrics and also on what they considered their personal integrity. Several of the men midwives said that they could not possibly be responsible for carrying infection from one patient to another.[10]

By 1869, Johnston was master at the Rotunda and felt under particular attack about puerperal fever. Anxious to avoid any charge of mismanagement, he introduced a new line of argument in his first annual clinical report, in 1869, where he listed twenty-five maternal deaths. It was here he first advanced the rationale that those women who had contracted puerperal fever had done so because as victims of 'seduction,' they were already weakened by 'remorse and fretting'. Thus they had been unable to withstand the rigours of childbirth and consequently developed the fever. His opening remarks were a defence of the hospital system in general. He claimed that any infectious fevers which appeared in the hospital were ones for which women had a propensity because of where they lived and which they brought with them:

How much rather should we look for these diseases in the localities from those seeking admission emanate, in the narrow, filthy, unswept streets, the courts and alleys in too many instances reeking with pestilential effluvia of half-putrid offal and ordure, which by imperfect sewage or no sewage at all, allows the noxious gases escaping therefrom to pervade the overcrowded, small, unwashed, ill-ventilated apartments, their bedding, if possessed of such a luxury, saturated with filth and dirt; the unfortunate occupants frequently in a weak, emaciated state, from want, penury, starvation and disease ... in fact everything most likely to engender the malady we all have so much to fear. (Johnston, 1870)

The conditions in which working class women lived did not cover all instances of puerperal fever, so Johnston supplemented it with inferences about the deadly consequences of promiscuous sexual behaviour. In his list of maternal deaths, he made entries under the heading 'Cause' like:

Pyaemia	*Victim of seduction, remorse*
	and fretting extreme
Peritonitus	*Ditto*
Mental Shock	*Ditto*
Mental Shock	*Seduction, great mental depression*

The fuller case notes added this detail:

No.4. 25 years of age, her first pregnancy and died of pyaemia, 15th day after delivery. She was admitted from a distant county, the victim of seduction, and her remorse and fretting from the moment of coming in was extreme and most distressing to witness.

No.35 34 years of age. She also was the victim of seduction, distress of mind and remorse no doubt being the cause of the fatal illness.

No.12 28 years of age, second pregnancy, unmarried, caught cold in a railway train coming up from County Meath, was lying in a lodging house for a week ... Peritoneal symptoms set in immediately after delivery, between which and distress of mind she sank on the fourth day. (Johnston, 1870)

The phrase 'she sank' sounds quite gentle yet it obscured the horror of a death from puerperal fever in which women endured agonising pain while remaining conscious and articulate until their last few moments alive.

The etiology of puerperal fever was simple enough.[11] What men midwives described as puerperal fever or peritonitus (they used these terms interchangeably) they associated with only the one symptom of distended and extremely painful abdomen. In fact their definition of puerperal fever was only one manifestation of an enormous range of illnesses like pyaemia, erysipelas, and phlebitis, which, beginning with obstetrically induced infection in the uterus, often ended in women's deaths. Bacteria would spread from the initial site of infection in the uterus either into the abdominal cavity, or into the bloodstream, or would trigger the formation of infected clots in the pelvic veins, or inflame pelvic connective tissue. These serious puerperal infections frequently overwhelmed the body's defences and ended in death. There were three sources of obstetrically-induced infection. The first was the septic environment of the hospital itself, a far greater threat to women than the slums.[12] Secondly, there were the hands of the men midwives as they examined women which spread infection to the uterus either from other women or from the dissecting room. The third source of infection comprised the torn and bruised tissues of the cervix and vagina in the wake of a mechanical obstetric intervention like a forceps delivery.

What is clear is that at least twenty-three of the twenty-five maternal deaths which Johnston recorded in his first annual report were attributable to obstetrically-induced infection. The clinical records reveal the process whereby the cause of death was filtered through the pre-existing model of women that men midwives had created. When women died after childbirth from infectious disease, that disease was seen to have a causal relationship to the model of how women were thought to function rather than to their management by men midwives. Men midwives disclaimed responsibility by explaining that death in childbirth was part of the physical susceptibility of being a woman. Further disclaimers could be attached to poor women coming in from the slums, that they brought the disease in with them. But a novel extension of the incompetent female model was Johnston's labelling of unmarried women as being most susceptible to fever. In his subsequent clinical reports, Johnston wrote at length about the women he called 'innupta', that is unmarried, saying that such women were 'admitted in a state of great mental distress from seduction.' It was à 'notorious fact,' he commented, 'that whenever they found feverish symptoms occurring after delivery, they constantly traced them to mental anxiety, caused either by seduction or by the husband having deserted and beaten his wife.' (Johnston, 1872)

The common perception of the process of labour amongst men midwives was that it should always be in their control. They cited overwhelming pain, the baby acting as a battering ram against the 'soft parts', and women's general tendency to disease as reasons why they should intervene. So despite the individual pattern of each woman's labour, all were made to conform to an invariable rule. If first stage labour, when the cervix was dilating, was slower than men midwives wished, they forced the pace by employing both manual dilation of the cervix with their fingers and a mechanical dilator. The expulsive second stage they could terminate with forceps. Such interventions also introduced the opportunity for infection. Thus a woman who laboured slowly for whatever reason was particularly at risk in contracting puerperal fever as a result of her management by men midwives.

Johnston became convinced that these slow labours were more likely to occur amongst unmarried women because of their overwrought emotional state, and that in instances such as these, he should use the forceps to terminate labour rapidly.[13] He reasoned that this would protect women from inflammation and fever:

Why should we permit a fellow-creature to undergo hours of torture when we have the means of relieving her within our reach? Why should she be allowed to waste her strength and incur the risks consequent upon the long pressure of the head on the soft parts ... one of the fertile causes of puerperal fever (is) the labour being allowed to continue till inflammatory symptoms appear. (Johnston, 1872)

The application of the forceps he argued was a 'timely interference' which would bring benefits to both women and babies, lowering mortality rates. In his annual account for 1872, he reported that he had used the forceps on 131 women, nine of whom had died from puerperal fever. On thirty-five of these women, he had employed the forceps when they were as little as two-fifths dilated, that is, when the cervix was less than half open. Claiming this as a new practice not reported before in midwifery annals, Johnston wrote that he had adopted it after a case in which a woman exhibited 'symptoms ... such as to induce him to deliver with the forceps ... She went on favourably until the third day when on going round the wards,' he found her 'in a state of collapse and she passed away'. The post-mortem revealed that the cervix had become completely detached and had been sloughed off. However, Johnston did not interpret this as a consequence of his hasty forceps operation but said the woman's case 'had induced him to adopt the practice he had followed ever since (applying the forceps before full dilation) and he found it attended with the greatest advantage, both to the safety of the mother and the child' (Johnston, 1872). To prove his point about the efficacy of the forceps, he described in detail another case in which he delivered a woman by forceps before she was fully dilated. When he found he could expand her cervix with his finger, he did not hesitate to use the forceps. Her death shortly thereafter was free of any uterine symptoms, he wrote. Johnston's reasoning about using forceps is a prime example of the male medical model about women. He was able to view the deaths as extraneous detail, unconnected with the intervention, because he had fulfilled his task of rescuing women from the danger of labour.

A master of the Rotunda holds office for seven years in which time he lays down the obstetric policy of the hospital. By the time Johnston completed his mastership in 1875, the number of forceps deliveries was higher than at any other point in the nineteenth century. He had sanctioned their use in 752 women out of 7,862; 554 of these were first time-mothers; 123 women had had the forceps applied to them before full dilation had occurred, of whom 44 had been subjected to the forceps when only two-fifths dilated. The mortality rate was greatest amongst the women who had been least dilated when the forceps were applied. Johnston's statistics indicate that the woman who was allowed to labour without forceps had one chance in 233 of contracting puerperal fever in comparison with a woman delivered by forceps who faced a one in fifteen chance.

Altogether, forty-eight women of the first-time mothers subjected to forceps died after they gave birth, from puerperal fever. Of these forty-eight, Johnston wrote that twenty-eight developed puerperal fever because they were unmarried women suffering as a result of their seduction.

In his summary clinical report on the use of forceps, presented to the Dublin Obstetrical Society in 1878, he maintained that delivery by forceps especially before full dilation was 'perfectly safe and its use justifiable for it ... in great measure secures the safety of the mother ... by obviating the danger produced by prolonged pressure of the foetal head on the maternal soft parts, and all of its evil consequences.' (Johnston, 1879)

Working from the incompetent female model, Johnston had employed an obstetric technique which actually substantially increased the risk of maternal mortality. The practice, based on this model, determined the adverse birth outcomes of the women subjected to a forceps delivery.

The Invention of Women's Identity as Childbearers

In examining how power and knowledge function through discourse, Foucault has written that medicine surrounds itself with a 'solid scientific armature' (1980). Yet at the same time medical discourse, playing a key role in bio-politics, has been profoundly implicated in the production of social relations. This medical armature enabled the forceps policy to be carried out in the Rotunda. The scientificity of Johnston's clinical accounts served to disguise how women were subjected to a set of power relations which they could not challenge.

By the 1870s, the Rotunda had enjoyed an international reputation in obstetric practice for more than 100 years. Its clinical records were treated as an ongoing authoritative source of the hospital's teaching on the management of childbirth. Johnston himself was praised by his colleagues for being a skilful, earnest clinician who exercised careful judgement along with manual dexterity. He was not an aberration outside the medical paradigm but worked from solidly within it. His ideas were not new amongst men midwives. The attribution of a death from puerperal fever to a woman's emotional state, citing her presumed grief and shame about her pregnancy, had been advanced before.

Nor was it unheard of to apply the forceps to women when they were only partially dilated. Despite his boast, Johnston had been preceded in advocating this practice by the British man midwife, Smellie, 125 years earlier.[14]

The power of men midwives to impose practices arbitrarily stemmed from their theoretical discourses. Once these discourses had secured expression through the institution of the lying-in hospital, it was inevitable that men midwives would invent the necessity for obstetric practices without having to question their effects on women. Johnston's policy on forceps is one example of how this power worked. He was able to sanction the use of forceps on a wide scale, tying it to his theory about women and seduction, and the need to absolve the hospital from any responsibility in creating puerperal fever epidemics.

After Johnston gave his final paper on forceps deliveries to the Dublin Obstetrical Society in 1878, his colleagues debated the issue almost exclusively in terms of whether the increased use of forceps would lower maternal mortality rates and so advance the hospital's teaching reputation. When referred to in debate, the objects of this practice, the women, appeared most frequently as numbers, averages, and fractions of the many statistics presented to 'prove' lower mortality, emphasising how essential demographic techniques and a numerical discourse were to the politics of male midwifery.

In both Johnston's clinical reports and the debates on them, women were treated as a distinct population presenting a series of technical problems which were dealt with by breaking them down into subcategories of cases and characteristics, all of which were specified by men midwives. The numbering and categorising of pregnant women was one of the mechanisms of objectification around which the power relations were organised within the lying-in hospital. Like the staff at the French penitentiary, Mettary, whom Foucault describes as 'technicians of behaviour' (1979), the men midwives also created a set of power relations through an interlocking series of techniques and discursive mechanisms to produce docile bodies. In a similar manner, the clinical reports of the Rotunda function as a discursive mechanism.

Johnston's colleagues never questioned the central premise about the weakness of women in childbirth, and his seduction theory was an acceptable explanation of death from puerperal fever amongst the group of unmarried women. Throughout Johnston's mastership, the only hesitation in classifying women as having been seduced was whether prostitutes might be masquerading as genuine victims of seduction in order to seek shelter in the hospital when giving birth.

The forceps era in the Rotunda provides a graphic illustration of the continuity of power relations which have enmeshed women in childbirth since the eighteenth century. In this instance, unmarried women were made into a specific medical problem and labelled as victims, which resulted in their being further victimised with, for them, disastrous consequences.

In examining male ideologies about women, MacKinnon (1982) observes that the elements which compose the female stereotype reflect male sexual power. The imputed quality of female passivity for example, reflects the male expectation of a lack of resistance which is reinforced by social practices. So also, female incompetence summons up male support albeit on male terms. An examination of obstetric discourse reveals the process of male ideology about women's bodies in the making. From the time when male medical discourses first defined the female body in labour as problematic, women were mapped out as territory where obstetric practices could be endlessly rehearsed and a discourse was further developed to legitimate these practices. Men midwives laid claim to the territory of the female body through the invention of their theory about female incompetence.

It has meant that women undergoing childbirth have been subject to a definition of themselves which originated within male medical discourse. This definition has had concrete effects on women and continues to permeate obstetric thinking.[15] Obstetric theory and practice have modified both the identity of women as childbearers and their birth outcomes. Freud wrote in *Dora*: 'I will simply claim myself the rights of the gynaecologist - or rather much more modest ones.' It is little wonder that Freud aspired to even some of the unlimited power that men midwives had. Their ability to dominate the female body in labour by means of the obstetric view of feminine identity has led to their total control of women's reproductive care.

Jo Murphy-Lawless
1988

Notes

1. See for instance Brook (1976), Kitzinger (1979), Beels (1978), and Inch (1983).
2. On the history of male-controlled childbirth see Arms, 1975, 1977; Ehrenreich and English (1973); Oakley (1976); Donnison (1977); Rich (1977); Wertz and Wertz (1977); and Versluysen (1981).
3. Given that the baby's head moves down the birth canal stretching the perineum only very gradually, there is no logical rationale for this image of a battering ram. See Mehl, Peterson, and Brandsel, 'Episiotomy, Facts, Figures and Alternatives' in D and L Stewart (eds.) *Compulsory Hospitalization or Freedom of Choice in Childbirth?*
4. Foucault discusses medical practice emerging as part of the apparatus of collective control of the body in 'The Politics of Health in the eighteenth Century' in *Power/Knowledge* C Gordon, (ed). See also 'The Confessions of the Flesh,' ibid.
5. This opinion, expressed by a well-known Dublin preacher, Dr Lawson, in his sermon to mark the opening of the chapel to the Rotunda in 1759, was the main reason for the public support the Rotunda received from the outset. See its *Royal Charter 1756*. That women from the class of the 'labouring poor' were assigned a pivotal role as reproducers is clear from the large amount of state aid granted to the Rotunda by the Irish House of Commons throughout the eighteenth century. For perceptions about poverty in eighteenth century Ireland, see C Maxwell, *Dublin Under the Georges 1714-1830* (1956) and L Cullen, *An Economic History of Ireland Since 1660* (1972).

6. Irish scientists in the eighteenth century saw the expansion of medical practice as a way of establishing a reputation at international level they did not otherwise possess because of their colonial status in relation to mainland Britain. In 1757, the Medico-Philosophical Society exhorted doctors to take up 'their duty to publish the results of the experiences for the benefit of others in the fields of anatomy, physiology, surgery and midwifery.' See *Transactions, Medical and Philosophical Memoirs*, Volume 1, 1757, Medico-Philosophical Society.

7. The Wertzes in their history of childbirth management in America speak of puerperal fever as a 'classic example of iatrogenic disease' (1977).

8. An early master of the Rotunda, Dr Joseph Clarke, claimed he had never encountered a case of puerperal fever in any of his private patients over thirty-five years.

9. 'There are two main sources of mortality in the Rotunda Hospital. One large source arises from the number of unmarried women ... the other is the immense number of primipararous cases' (first-time mothers), Dr McClintock, a former Master of the Rotunda, stated in 1872. He argued that because it was a charity, the Rotunda was forced to accept a disproportionate number of women in these two categories. See 'Clinical Report of the Rotunda Lying-in Hospital, 1871'. The medical opinion that most deaths could not be attributed to hospital practices but to the physical and emotional state of women prior to their entry was repeatedly aired in discussions about peurperal fever.

10. Although men midwives readily viewed unmarried women's social circumstances as a moral issue which entailed physiological consequences, they refused to examine whether they themselves had any personal culpability in causing puerperal fever. Their status as professionals left them above suspicion, they argued.

11. See Shorter's *History of Women's Bodies*.

12. Again, Shorter makes the point that maternal mortality was far less common in homes no matter how unfavourable the conditions, because working-class women acquired a degree of immunity to their own bacteria whereas the hospital exposed them to 'spectacular insalubrity'.

13. In *Practical Midwifery*, Johnston had made the distinction between 'tedious' labours which were simply slow according to the men midwives, and difficult labours where the forceps or other instruments had to be used because labour was clearly impeded by gross pelvic deformity, for instance, as a result of rickets. Johnston had merged the two categories by the time he became master, so that a slow labour, a common enough occurrence with first-time mothers, became classed as dangerous. Hence Johnston was inclined to treat first-time mothers as he did unmarried women.

14. Obstetric history is rife with similar examples. In American hospital, De lee's system of prophylactic forceps deliveries, in combination with the notorious drug scopolamine, enjoyed great popularity from the 1920s onwards. See J De Lee, 'The prophylactic forceps operation,' *American Journal of Obstetrics and Gynaecology 1*, October, 1920. Also see Kitzinger (1985). For an account of De lee's influence on obstetric practice in America, see W. Arney, *Power and the Profession of Obstetrics* (1983). For nineteenth century examples of American medical arguments on women's emotional instability in childbirth, see G J Barker-Benfield, *The Horrors of the Half-Known Life* (1976).

15. A telling instance of women's objectification appeared in the 1985 annual report for St James Hospital in Dublin: as reported in the *Irish Medical Times*, January, 1986, 'St James is indebted to the Coombe Hospital for taking a number of very premature in uteri transfers of babies.' The pregnant women who were moved from one hospital to another are here referred to only by the phrase 'in utero,' as passive baby carriers.

The Struggle for Reproductive Rights
A Brief History in its Political Context

When we examine Irish history and the events that have shaped women's lives, we note the important fact that Irish people as a whole did not have control of our own destiny: we have been an occupied nation and a colonised people. This fact of history has social and political consequences which prevented the emergence of secular social and independent political and economic institutions and structures. This overall underdevelopment prevented the emergence within civil society of a strong 'public sphere'. The 'public sphere' is typically the product of the interaction of the contradictory clashes between democratic forces in society (trade unions, working-class political parties, sections of the liberal intelligentsia, the women's movement, struggles for basic democratic rights) and the dominant political and economic institutions of independent capitalism. The emergence of these forces in developed capitalist economies is usually paralleled by the emergence of socialist organisations and political parties.

In an underdeveloped society the achievement of political independence (or partial independence in our case) does not bring into spontaneous existence all the features stultified by imperialism. In fact a vacuum exists, into which step traditionalist conservative forces who have been associated - in public consciousness if not in fact - with the nationalist movement. These social forces, in Ireland the Roman Catholic Church, are ones whose social institutions were encouraged or have at least benefited from forms of sometimes malign toleration during the last period of imperialist control.

In the event, it was the conservative side of the independence movement who were on the winning side in Ireland in 1921. They emerged victorious from the Civil War by becoming Britain's allies in the process of defeating the Republican forces. The incoming Cumann na nGael government began constructing a conservative state which reflected and entrenched the social values of the Roman Catholic Church. The minority Protestant Churches were predominantly upper-class institutions, only marginally less conservative than their Catholic counterparts on some questions. They were pleased with the outcome of the Civil War as it represented the victory of 'the lesser of two evils'. They were, in any case, utterly discredited as the spokespersons for the Anglo-Irish aristocracy and the British colonisers. Their 'democratic' credentials were such as to hinder rather than enhance any calls for democratic rights they might consider throwing their limited weight behind. An era of social reaction ensued, in which forces most likely to promote democratic advance were in effect politically liquidated by their defeat and suppression during and after the Civil War.

There is no doubt that the social institutions and ideology represented by the Catholic Church and promoted by successive governments stepped into the vacuum created by the absence of an indigenous public sphere and helped to further retard secular social progress. Prior to independence for the 26 County state, women had been active in the suffragette and nationalist movements. They saw no distinction between the fight against the British occupation and the fight for independence and women's rights.

A certain degree of autonomy for women, through the availability of contraception and a protracted divorce process, was the consequence of the victory of democratic forces in Britain itself which were incidentally transferred to Ireland. Forms of contraception were common to the indigenous culture of Irish women who also performed infanticide during the nineteenth century. The victory of a repressive sexual morality imposed by the Catholic Church under Cardinal Cullen during the second half of the nineteenth century was seen by the Cardinal as a means of disciplining the Catholic masses, bringing them under the increasingly repressive sway of Rome and curtailing the radical influence of secular Republican ideas. Sexual liberty was cleverly portrayed by the Church as a form of peculiarly British 'godlessness' and used to harness legitimate anti-British feeling for the purposes of promoting Catholic ideology. This 'consciousness-lowering' undoubtedly had an effect on the more conservative sections of the nationalist movement.

The 1920s witnessed draconian censorship of films and publications in Ireland. Legislation was aimed both at depictions of sexuality and at preventing the 'spread' of communism. Curtailing the spread of radical social and political ideas went hand in hand. These measures could be portrayed as a means of protecting Irish particularity - the equation of nationality and religion being one of the ideological tenets of the new state. The process of obtaining a divorce through a petition to the British House of Lords was abolished. A prohibition on the importation and sale of contraceptives ensued in 1935, despite the energetic opposition of women who had been active in the suffragette and nationalist movements, and who retained their republican consciousness. Much has been written about Protestant Church opposition to banning contraception. However, as well as recognising the limited credibility of this institution, it is important to point out the reactionary nature of aspects of the Protestant promotion of contraception which was seen as a means of preventing the 'over-breeding' of the Catholic masses rather than as a democratic liberty in its own right. Such a characteristically Ascendancy outlook was hardly likely to win over an already sceptical public opinion.

The women's movement in Ireland was marginalised by the victory of reaction both in Ireland and in Europe generally in the 1920s and 1930s. Eamonn de Valera's more rhetorically radical Fianna Fáil came to power in 1932 - and remained there until 1948 - on a wave of working-class and small farmer support. Fianna Fáil pursued a policy of indigenous capitalist economic development aimed at building an industrial base and sustaining the agricultural population. This economic populism, which incidentally received the support of John Maynard Keynes in 1934, consolidated working-class support while retaining the support of the poorer farmers by building up industrial employment and a policy of public house-building. While being less conservative than Cumann na nGael (then in the process of decomposition into the fascist Blueshirts before re-emerging as Fine Gael) in terms of economic policy, Fianna Fáil was only marginally less so (if at all) in terms of social policy.

After passing the 1935 law against contraception de Valera's 1937 Constitution gave official recognition to the retreat of women from public life into 'work in the home' by such measures as the ban on divorce and the aforementioned notorious 'need' to prevent economic 'coercion' from 'forcing' women into the workplace. The infamous recognition of the 'special place' of the Catholic Church was in fact opposed by the Catholic Church, since it also gave recognition to other Churches. However, as with most social facts, the Constitution was a contradictory document. Articles 2 and 3 gave political recognition, if not effect, to the democratic aspiration to Irish control over the whole island of Ireland, while a limited form of a Bill of Rights allowed democratic reform which eventually declared the 1935 contraception law partially unconstitutional in 1973 and declared men-only juries unconstitutional in 1974. On the whole, though, the Constitution copperfastened a period of social reaction and isolationism, since Catholic control of educational, health and other social institutions continued unabated. The economic and social isolationism of this period can be viewed as part of a process of partitionist 'nation building'. The last public gasp of the coalition of Republican women and other women activists occurred when they attempted to defeat the 1937 Constitution referendum which passed by a small majority.

After the vicissitudes of the 'Emergency' in the period 1939-45, which witnessed increased repression through internment, censorship, military courts and executions, Fianna Fáil's grip on popular support was slipping. Increasing emigration and unemployment further alienated public opinion. After the 1940s, a process which has become familiar to us today began to emerge. There were skirmishes centering around Catholic control of social policy which were combined with the increasingly atrophied attempts by successive governments to maintain social peace while failing to tackle the Church's increasingly obsolete ideological control over society.

In 1948 a radical new republican party, Clann na Poblachta, came to power in coalition with Fine Gael and other parties. The Clann was led by a former Chief of Staff of the IRA in the 1930s, Seán MacBride, who became Minister for External Affairs. The Minister for Health was Clann member, Noel Browne, who is credited with abolishing the scourge of tuberculosis. Browne energetically followed this success with the now famous Mother and Child scheme. Among other things, this proposed social reform encouraged or allowed family or other doctors to advise mothers on such things as family size.

Browne's proposal outraged the Catholic Church which correctly saw it as the thin end of a wedge prising women away from total reliance on Catholic teaching in regard to family matters. This challenge to its ideological authority and power base caused the organisation of a clerical-government *coup* against Browne, who was sacked. On the central issue of encouraging secular advance a second rhetorically reformist republican leader, MacBride, would only go so far and then he retreated. In the ensuing election of 1951 Fianna Fáil returned to power. The Clann gradually disappeared from public view and disintegrated. Fianna Fáil brought in a watered down version of the Mother and Child scheme.

Fianna Fáil was out of power again from 1954 to 1957 and then remained in power until 1973. The 1950s was a period of increasing economic decline and social stagnation. The ability of the society to sustain itself was questioned as population decline continued. Social stultification was the order of the day as protected and unplanned capitalist economic development exhausted the possibilities of an impoverished local market while not generating sufficient economic growth. A society which banned the books of the world's leading writers, including its own, which banned films with abandon and which could not provide for its own population was viewed with increasing incredulity by its own citizens and by foreign observers.

This was a crisis for the ruling class, which understood the social and political portents heralded by the election of four Sinn Féin and two unemployment candidates in the 1957 election. The policy of economic protectionism was finally officially abandoned, having been largely ignored for many years. A new policy of foreign multinational investment was encouraged. The 1960s was a period when economic growth resulted from the state enjoying the benefits of the last gasp of the worldwide economic boom lasting from 1945 to 1973, which had eluded us previously because of a refusal by the major economies to allow the protected Irish economy to participate fully in the world market. This policy was paralleled in the 1960s by the setting up of Irish television whose increasingly liberal outlook was encouraged by a worldwide wave of protest against the USA invasion of Vietnam, the discrimination against Black people in the USA and in South Africa. The modern Women's Liberation Movement was also emerging internationally.

These protest movements had an effect on a new radical interpretation of the failures of the Irish state on the occasion of the fiftieth anniversary of the 1916 Rising in 1966. The socialist republicanism of the 1916 leader, James Connolly, re-emerged, as did his considerable writings and action on behalf of female suffrage and employment rights. International and local pressures affected the formation of the Civil Rights Movement in the North (which opposed a pro-British semi-dictatorship), the Women's Movement in the South and other movements for social reform in the South. The social reality of 'churching' women after childbirth, forcing single women to give up children for adoption, notorious Church-run mother and child homes, the ban on contraception and divorce, the absence of women on juries, the ban on married women in the civil service - all of these social barbarisms were a growing indictment of a society increasingly claiming an equal place in the modern and developed world. In 1970 over 1,000 women gathered for a rally in the Mansion House in

Dublin. As well as political pressure groups, women's growing activity also generated the provision of services which the state was incapable or unwilling to provide.

There was a three-fold combination of a youth radicalisation, a women's radicalisation and a Republican radicalisation all challenging the legitimacy of the Irish state's policies. Reforms came in a piecemeal and distorted fashion. Formally free secondary education was inaugurated in the eventful year of 1968 - the only substantial undiluted response to social pressure to emerge in the past twenty-five years. The 1970s was a period of considerable activity. In 1972 a Commission on the Status of Women was set up. In 1973 the people voted down the Constitutional and largely symbolic 'special position' of the Catholic Church. The 1973 *McGee* case introduced contraceptive reform.

Irish Women United and the appropriately named Contraception Action Programme (CAP) - both of which I was a member - had a considerable effect with direct action activities: opening illegal contraception shops and stalls and occupying the Federated Union of Employers' HQ when they opposed the introduction of Equal Pay, for example. The 1973-77 Coalition (Fine Gael plus Labour) agreed to the Federated Union of Employers', request to 'postpone' equal pay laws. This activity outraged the mass of Irish women who demonstrated in their thousands. The EEC responded to the pressure and forced the government to bring in equal pay legislation. This result of the effect of mass action is often portrayed as the beneficial bequest of the EEC, whereas the catalyst and cause was the activity of radical women's groups and the mass of Irish women.

During the 1960s and increasingly throughout the 1970s individual doctors and clinics began dispensing both contraceptive advice and contraceptives. Pope Paul's 1968 encyclical reaffirming the ban on so-called 'unnatural' contraception was increasingly ignored. The advent of the 'Pill', which in principle liberated sexual activity from the threat of unplanned pregnancy, put the control, but also the onus, of contraception more firmly in women's hands. The IUD was available and availed of mostly by working-class women increasingly determined to avoid the 'traditional' experience of extremely large Catholic families. The fiction of prescribing female contraceptives as menstrual 'cycle regulators' was widespread.

The fight for free, legal contraception was increasingly part of a struggle for basic democratic rights and escaped from its previous incarnation in the 1930s as an elite (viewed as Protestant) form of 'population control'. Secular mass action by women of Catholic origin, if not any longer of that orientation, was bringing Church and State law into disrepute. The 'Pill Train' from Belfast saw women dispensing contraceptives to eager hands reaching over ineffective customs barriers in the aptly-named Connolly Train Station in Dublin. The 1973 Supreme Court decision allowed the personal importation of contraceptives for private use while maintaining the ban on sale. After a series of legislative fiascoes (in which a Fine Gael Taoiseach (Prime Minister) and Minister for Education voted against their own government's idiotic bill in 1974) it took another ten years before reform finally merely allowed the sale of condoms from pharmacies.

While radicalisation on the North was curtailed through a policy of censorship, propaganda and repression, women's radicalisation was more difficult to contain. Campaigning on the disgraceful inadequacies within southern society provided an increasingly effective alternative outlet for radical energies. It also led to an unfortunate isolationist attitude in relation to reform in the South, while abandoning the North. Women in the northern ghettos, and their radicalisation, were largely either dismissed or ignored. Conservative voices within Irish feminism encouraged this outlook and encouraged a new social orthodoxy which equated the struggle for self-determination itself as part of the backwardness of Irish society. In truth, that backwardness is a result of the combination of partial victory and defeat which emerged from the 1921 settlement - partial political independence combined with a massive social conservatism which maintained and consolidated that victory for backward social forces. These social forces were and are those most anxious to repress moves toward questioning the 1921 settlement. Today, the 'revisionist' history which portrays the legacy of British imperialism as a 'civilising' influence on the savage Irish mind now also tends to compare the EC with what we would do if left to our own devices. What is always left out of this equation is the mass action of the Irish people, including that of Irish women. Mass political action itself forced and wrenched reforms from governments on the continent of Europe. That is the legacy of history which censorship increasingly obscures. It is part of the history which Irish women must reclaim. However, even that is not sufficient; you can only live on a legacy for so long. The benefits of a political legacy are based on the struggles of the past. They will eventually dissipate if not reinvested in new political energy and struggles.

While reform was also apparent in the context of liberalisation of censorship of publications and films it was increasing in the context of RTE's political reporting and particularly its reporting of the 'troubles' in the North. In 1969 the Government under Jack Lynch had set up a public enquiry into an RTE *Seven Days'* report on illegal and legal money-lending, a scourge of the working class to the benefit of rich and 'respectable' Irish financiers who were the real support base of Fianna Fáil. To the amazement of observers from abroad this enquiry was not into the evil of money-lending itself but into the so-called 'illegitimate' reporting techniques of the broadcasters. In 1971 the Government instituted political censorship of reporting of the North. This process was consolidated in those more obstreperous times by the dismissal of an entire RTE Authority and the efforts of a juryless Special Criminal Court which sentenced a journalist, Kevin O'Kelly, to three months' imprisonment for contempt when he refused to identify an IRA spokesperson on a taped interview. Later in 1976, Conor Cruise O'Brien, as part of a new Coalition 'Kulturkamp', reinforced Section 31 censorship even further and produced even more timidity within RTE.

The late 1970s and the early 1980s witnessed a decline in direct action as the previous radicalisation exhausted itself. Economic factors which resulted in growing unemployment and a return of emigration on a massive scale encouraged social demoralisation. Conservative feminists identified Fine Gael as a vehicle for social reform - such was the pathetic level of historical consciousness of these forces. They retreated into the mirage of Fine Gael feminism; the international and indigenous right was remobilising. A conservative Polish pope with a mission visited Ireland in 1979 and reinvigorated the social base of conservative Catholicism. This was a secular phenomenon - the head of the Roman Catholic Church, Cardinal Tomás Ó Fiaich, was largely indifferent to the paranoia of the conservative Catholic intelligentsia and was either indifferent to or incapable of combating secular influences. He was also less inclined to bow to British repression in the North. For this unique disability Ó Fiaich suffered a propaganda barrage from the southern Government and media - who are largely relieved by his successor, very much the opposite to Ó Fiaich.

The epitome of the inadequacies of Irish liberalism, the Fine Gael Taoiseach, Dr Garret FitzGerald, who was reeling from the republican radicalisation resulting from the H-Block hunger strikes in the early 1980s, acquiesced to a demand by the newly formed Irish version of SPUC in 1983 by agreeing to a Constitutional ban on abortion - which was already illegal. The Labour leader, Frank Cluskey, followed suit, as did Fianna Fáil's Charles Haughey. There had been no great debate on abortion. All that most Irish people knew about it was the international horror stories told by the ubiquitous Father Marx with his foetus in a jam jar which he carted around most of the religious-controlled secondary schools. Father Marx was given free reign on RTE's *Late Late Show* (Ireland's major television talk show) which was later banned from holding a sober debate on the consequences of the proposal to ban abortion constitutionally. Abortion, like the North, was the great taboo subject. Certain Fine Gael 'feminist' TDs were seen with the badge of foetal respectability, SPUC's *little feet* lapel pin.

FitzGerald later attempted to rehabilitate himself when

he unsuccessfully tried to amend the initial and eventually successful referendum wording. The real opposition to SPUC came from a coalition of the emerging liberal intelligentsia and the various strands of the autonomous women's movement. It is true that in the early 1980s women's groups had begun to tentatively raise the question of abortion and the fact that increasing numbers of Irish women were going to England to avail of its more liberal abortion laws. There was abortion in Ireland, they said, except that it physically took place in England. These women had and have a right to escape social ostracism. Their experiences and histories were and are part of the history of Irish women. These women were entitled to non-directive counselling by women who would not condemn or censor or interfere with their decision.

After the referendum was passed by a 70:30 majority - the 30 per cent itself an achievement by an opposition with little resources fighting a combination of social hysteria and the social might of Fianna Fáil, the utter disarray of the other Leinster House parties, the Catholic Church and the radicalised ignorance of sections of the Catholic masses - the SPUC ideologues turned their attention to the non-directive counselling which continued to exist. The legal limbo women counsellors inhabited was curtailed by the Supreme Court which declared the Well Woman Centre and Open Line Counselling to be abortion referral agencies and therefore to be in contravention of the abortion ban. Censorship of information on abortion also ensued from the decision, in which the media meekly acquiesced. It was the Union of Students in Ireland (USI) which then took up the fight and fought a ban on publishing abortion information advice and telephone numbers. The students, with a new radical young leadership, ignored Supreme Court rulings to desist from publication. Just as in the 1970s, it was independent and radical forces which stood out from prevailing orthodoxy and helped regalvanise opposition to social conservatism.

The period of reaction continued, however, when, in a cynical attempt to stave off a looming election defeat, FitzGerald tried to salvage his liberal reputation by holding an ill-considered and ill-fated referendum in 1986, proposing to end the ban on divorce. It was lost through a process of government unpopularity and a failure to recognise the economic inferiority of women who felt threatened by the measure, opposition from Fianna Fáil and the resurgent mobilisation of the radical right. The result of the divorce referendum demonstrated an inability to deliver basic social reform, even in the limited form offered by FitzGerald. The liberal intelligentsia also got its fingers badly burned when it put its faith in Fine Gael once more in the course of the campaign and did not distance itself sufficiently from an unpopular government.

The 1990s faced the 26 Counties with the challenge of AIDS and the inadequacies of the state's response. The lack of official concern with the extent of illegal drug use in working-class areas, the unavailability of adequate sex education, the continuing illegality of homosexuality, the Church's opposition to the wider availability of condoms, all threaten the social fabric and confront public consciousness with the inadequacies of the conservatism which underlies the basis of the state's existence.

The public conscience is also again confronted by the abortion question, this time in all its stark reality. At least 4,000 women a year have been silently having abortions in England since 1983, and the figure goes up relentlessly year after year. The real meaning of the Constitutional ban was brought home, however, in early 1992 when a raped fourteen-year-old pregnant girl was prevented by the Attorney General and the High Court from going to England for an abortion. Generalised and immediate outrage ensued as women in particular and many parents in general considered the action barbaric. The ban on abortion confronted the institution of the family and the rights of an individual girl demanding the right to control and end an enforced pregnancy. The travel ban was portrayed locally and internationally as a 'rapist's charter' and a form of 'state rape'. An immediate appeal to the Supreme Court reversed the ban on the basis of the equal right to life of the mother who, in this case, threatened suicide. The general prohibition on travel for the purpose

96

of obtaining an abortion was not reversed. In other words, Irish women are still denied, at the time of writing, the basic rights to travel and information. While one part of the abortion ban was relaxed with a liberal interpretation of the potential 'mother's' rights, another part put in place a draconian ban on a basic civil liberty.

The women's movement was outraged by the ban on travel while an increasingly paranoid SPUC, searching desperately for a theme with which to rehabilitate itself, charged that the Supreme Court decision allowed abortion right up to full term. A further complication ensued when it emerged that the government, in an effort to placate SPUC the previous year, had had inserted into the EC's Maastricht Treaty, an infamous secret Protocol which safeguarded Irish abortion laws from questioning by the European Court. This Protocol now seemed both to enshrine within EC law the ban on travel and to legitimate other parts of the Supreme Court decision. This Protocol, therefore, forced both sides of the abortion debate to oppose the Government in the Maastricht referendum in June 1992. In effect SPUC set out to use the referendum to remobilise its base through evermore lurid anti-abortion propaganda. While this cynical exercise might have raised the SPUC profile it severely harmed the radical opposition to Maastricht.

SPUC's association of its backward and reactionary ideas with calls for sovereignty and independence, as well as opposition to the end of Irish neutrality and the formation of a potential EC army served to partly confuse the 'No' side of the debate. The generally pro-EC media was only too happy to combine and confuse the SPUC arguments with rational arguments against Maastricht. In the end the Maastricht referendum was carried handsomely with many potential 'No' voters repelled by the presence of the so-called 'pro-life' presence on the opposition side - however inadvertently or unofficially. The anti-abortion side won no new forces to the anti-Maastricht position; if anything it deterred them. The media have allowed the SPUC activists to emerge, Svengali-like, from their campaign débâcle in order to put the case that the battle has 'only just begun' and that they were really involved in a mobilisation and propaganda exercise. They could not care less about Maastricht, as long as the Government gave them a new referendum proposing that the foetus be given new rights over and above those of the woman. While not publicly opposing the right to travel, SPUC will generate as much effort as appears necessary to retain the power to injunct women going abroad for abortions. The battle *is* only just beginning. Its resolution will determine the context for the fight for reproductive rights in years to come.

To conclude from this necessarily brief survey, I think it is clear firstly that the only way to win reform is to mobilise women for political action aimed at specific political ends. That is the lesson of the 1970s and, conversely, the lesson of the Right's mobilisation in the 1980s. Another lesson concerns the alacrity and complete unconcern manifested by EC leaders and bureaucrats when they agreed to the insertion of the anti-woman Protocol in the Maastricht Treaty. That action alone contradicts the notion that there is a 'reform mountain' within the EC which will modernise Irish society. Conservative Irish leaders want their clientelist economic position within the EC, accept economic subservience to the needs of multinationals, are prepared to subordinate indigenous economic structures to that end and, finally, wish to retain the conservative social structures which permeate the Irish state. The EC has proved itself happy to go along with this. Establishment political parties and other governments will not win rights for Irish women. Democratic reform will only be won through direct political action and the maximum amount of mass mobilisation possible.

Anne Speed
June 1992

The Death of Ann Lovett

Ann Lovett, aged 15, died giving birth in an open-air grotto, in Granard, on 31 January, 1984.

As in her pregnancy, so it was in her death. The people of Granard say with one voice: 'Ask the Family'. Ann Lovett's welfare was the inviolate responsibility of her parents. Had she or they asked outsiders for help it would have been forthcoming. So long as the family kept silent, the community honoured the unwritten code of non-interference with the basic unit of society.

'Even had I noticed she was pregnant,' says Canon Gilfillen, parish priest, 'I could hardly just come out and say "You're pregnant".' A businessman who once worked with the St Vincent de Paul says, 'Why do you think I left Saint Vincent's? The days when you could intervene are long gone. If a family doesn't want you to acknowledge that you know, there's nothing you can do. We knew Ann Lovett was pregnant. The family said nothing. If a family's broke these days you can't just offer them money. You can leave it secretly on the doorstep, but you can't go near them unless they ask.'

Diarmuid Lovett, father of nine and on the dole, is not broke in the sense of being entirely without standing. He has lived three years in Granard above his non-trading pub, The Copper Pot. He comes from a family of substance, the Lovetts, who used run a family building firm in nearby Kilnaleck. His brother John owns the Copper Kettle pub in Kilnaleck. Diarmuid Lovett is of sufficient standing in the area for his daughter's death to warrant a wreath from Kilnaleck Fianna Fáil Cumann (branch), and the attendance at her funeral of Mr John Wilson, Fianna Fáil TD from neighbouring Mullaghoran. Diarmuid Lovett is, by general reckoning, an abrupt, independent man.

People could hardly just come out and offer help that

might be misinterpreted as interference. It was assumed that the family knew and had made arrangements. Did the family know? 'Ask the Family,' says the community, leaving the Lovetts to cope full-frontally with the disaster. The twenty-two-year-old sister of Ann Lovett, with whom Ann spent some time in Dublin before Christmas, says, 'no comment'. The uncle of Ann Lovett says, 'Ask the Family', adding that it is the business of no one but the parents.

The Family sit behind the closed doors of the pub. Diarmuid and Patricia Lovett refuse to speak to reporters. The community will not, cannot, speak on their behalf. Canon Gilfillen says, 'I'd like to be able to help the family now but they've shut themselves away and seem to want to be alone. One's instinct is not to intrude.'

Ten days after Ann's death, the Gardaí (police) had not been able to secure an interview with her parents. Time is on their side, though, and they're playing a gentle waiting game. Soon, the Guards know - as the townspeople know, as the public knows, as the Church knows, as the Government which has instigated a private enquiry *via* the Departments of Health and Education knows - the parents must supply at least part of the answer. The death, in a public place, of a teenage girl and her newborn baby demands an attempt at explanation.

It will not be other than an ordeal for the two people of whom it will be demanded, her parents, who are her family. The townspeople cannot or will not help them bear that ordeal. It will be up to the family to explain how it could be that their daughter died unaided and alone. The efforts of the townspeople are directed towards explaining how they, the townspeople, could not come to her aid, though her condition was common knowledge.

More effort has been expended in defending the social superstructure than in defending the basic unit. The Convent of Mercy School, for example, called in a solicitor who, over a period of several hours, helped them draft a statement to the effect that the staff 'did not know' that Ann Lovett was pregnant. Did they, however, 'suspect' that she was? A spokeswoman, trembling and refusing to give her name, told *In Dublin* that the school would not comment on whether or not they suspected. They certainly 'did not know'. Nor would the school comment on the allegation that a teacher who could not stomach the nice legal distinction between 'knowing' and 'suspecting' refused to stand with the staff when the school statement was read out to *Today Tonight*.

If the school, under the authority of the headmistress Sister Maria, did not know or suspect anything, did the Convent, a separate institution in the same grounds, under the authority of Sister Immaculata, know or suspect that Ann Lovett was pregnant? (Convent sisters act as social workers in the town when they're not acting as teachers.) 'No comment.' Did Convent teachers, in their capacity as Convent sisters, approach the parents?' No comment.'

Eventually, with or without the solicitor's help, the school and the Convent will make a comment to their employers, the Department of Education. In the meantime, 'Ask the Family'.

While the Family wait alone for the inquisitional noose to tighten, while they wait for us who are not family to tighten it, the Gardaí pursue a duty which they describe as 'sickening'. A technical sexual offence has been committed, that of carnal knowledge with an under-age girl. They must interview the boyfriend with whom she had been keeping company for two years, until the relationship ended one month before she gave birth. His father is dead and his mother went to England last year. The boyfriend - 'Buddy' - lives in the family house, but he was in England during the summer. Did his summer begin in May, just before the pregnancy began, or later? Certainly, the Guards know he gave the key of his house to another youth who has left town since Ann Lovett died. Ann used to be seen coming out of that house. It would be a mercy to establish the line of paternity from there, whether or not prosecution ensues, because that would eliminate a third line of enquiry in a town and country now bursting with outspoken rumour.

'Buddy' has been, since Ann Lovett's death, visiting the Grotto wherein she gave birth on the moss-covered stone. By night he is to be found with other youths in the pool-halls, or pubs, for youth does not stay at home. On one such night, eleven nights after Ann Lovett's death, he stood in a pub with four of his pals, watching *The Late Late Show*. Gay Byrne was discussing pornography with an American woman of stout build. Her physical appearance drew the scorn of the youths.

Byrne ended the night by reviewing early editions of the weekend papers. The camera closed in on the semi-naked front-page woman in the *Sunday World*. 'I wouldn't mind having her,' said one of 'Buddy's' friends, and the others groaned assent. A studio guest criticised Mr Byrne for holding up the *Sunday World*. He replied that he was only reviewing the papers. She said the campaign against pornography was hopeless when such papers could be casually held up to view. 'She's right,' said one of the youths. They attempted a discussion of this point and couldn't sustain it. Gay Byrne had gone off the screen. The *Sunday World* couldn't be pornographic if it was a family Paper. 'Buddy' said nothing. The five boys went on to drink a little too much.

The conversation became raunchy. 'So I asked this girl to dance and held my cock right against her, like this' - the eldest boy demonstrated his body movements - 'and afterwards she looked me right in the eye, said thanks, and walked off the floor, the prick teaser.' The boys admired her cool cheek and regretted his bad luck. The discussion moved on to drink and which pint was the best brand. It was typical Saturday night peer-group conversation among young males. The youths made no connection between sexual activity and family consequences. 'Family' means married people, females and their babies.

Next morning during the Mass, Canon Gilfillen lashed out at the media for 'descending like locusts' to 'plague' and 'torment' the townspeople about a 'Family matter'. His sermon veered from a plea that it should be treated as such to a tirade against men committing adultery in their hearts when they lusted after women. And, he added, 'when divorce comes to the vote, as it surely will, we'll know where we stand. Against it, with the Church and with Christ.'

As for his teenage parishioners, a notice cut out of an *Irish Press* article on Ann Lovett's death has been tacked high up in a corner of the bulletin board in the Church porch. 'Where to find help', the newsprint reads. 'In pregnancy', has been pencilled in. They can find help anywhere but Granard, through Ally, Cherish and Cura, in Dublin, Kilkenny, Cork, Galway, Limerick, Waterford and Sligo, services for single mothers. No confidential telephone number in the town has been pencilled in.

Some of the services advertised use answering devices, which advise the caller to ring back. The services keep school hours. How often can you ring back from Granard's only public phone, in Main Street, when you should be in school, without attracting attention?

But then, Ann Lovett had attracted a lot of attention in her short lifetime.

'Wake up, Granard,' she used shout down Main Street after nightfall. Her father used to publicly pull her home from the grocery store-cum-billiard-hall where she spent much of her time. The sight of him and of her whom they knew to be pregnant, allayed concern as to who was taking responsibility for her welfare. 'He'd give her a cuff. Many a father does. You don't call in the ISPCC (Irish Society for the Prevention of Cruelty to Children), do you? If anything, you'd say he was doing his best, wouldn't you? And he'd be entitled to give you a cuff yourself if you stepped in. But why would you step in?'

The family looked all right. Ann Lovett looked properly fed and dressed and bright-eyed. The fact that she was pregnant besides was no reason for intervention. If there was a tension between her and her father, and there was, and if it was known, which it was, and if she spent a lot of time in the houses of her friends, what else could you expect in the circumstances? It was only natural, wasn't it?

That same Saturday night, in a pub in town, a group of middle-aged men and women, married to each other, had a relaxing drink. The barman produced a leaflet which occasioned laughter. 'Prick of the Week' read the legend under a pen-and-ink reproduction of a tumescent penis, complete with scrotum. 'Prick of the Week, for having made a balls-up is ...' read the mock certificate. It is up to the drinkers to fill in the name and the *faux pas* in question if they wish to engage in the pub joke.

A clear distinction was made between the joke and the tragedy of Ann Lovett, the mention of whose name brought an angrily defensive response. That was serious. This was funny. References to men and their sexuality is a joke, isn't it? Not to be connected with women, for Christ's sake. Just like the joke on last night's *Late Late* about children in nappies and the connection with pornography. Naked little boys and girls aren't the same as naked big boys and girls. Can we not make jokes, for Christ's sake? Gay Byrne has a sense of humour. They identify more with television than with Church.

On Monday, thirteen days after Ann Lovett's death, the spotlight swivelled on to another institution. The Guards were meeting in the station to co-ordinate procedure. Had a teenage boy been found dying from whatever cause, no-one would have baulked at an enquiry. You don't walk away from a male youth, found dying in a Grotto that celebrates the Virgin Birth. Nor can the Guards treat maternal death as an occurrence that is as natural or miraculous as conception, pregnancy and birth.

In the event, and in the panic, the other social units did. On the day of Ann Lovett's death nobody informed the Guards of the events in the Grotto. One of them, coming on duty at six in the evening, remarked that there were rumours in the town of an abortion. It was eight o'clock, three-and-a-half hours after Ann Lovett had been found, before the Guards established the facts, by dint of foot-slogging and telephone calls around the locality.

Doctor Tom Donohue, deputy coroner for the area, was a man well versed in the legal procedures that flow from the discovery of a dead body. It must not be moved. Doctor Donohue, who had treated Ann Lovett for shingles on her back shortly before Christmas, treated her as she lay dying in the Grotto. She was then moved by ambulance to Meath, out of the jurisdiction of Longford. The baby, which was dead and should not have been moved, was taken with her. Dr Donohue refused to comment on what was treated, in the circumstances, as a Family Affair.

Contrary to press reports, the Grotto where Ann Lovett gave birth - and where her baby died, where the priest gave her Extreme Unction and baptised the baby, where the doctor treated her, where her parents were brought to be with her - is not accessible to the public gaze. It is the most secluded spot in Granard town, which is why the young go there when they are mitching school. It lies just beyond, but enough beyond, the church and the row of houses opposite the church which mark the end of the town proper. Beyond the church and the houses, there is only a hill and beyond that along the deserted country road, there is only the graveyard.

Unless you turned sharp left up a broad, leafy, walled lane and stepped through a gate into a lonely quarried dell enclosed by a tall thicket. High up on the granite of the dell is the Virgin Mary. She can be seen from the public road, through the evergreen trees. A person lying on the ground at her feet would not be seen. A girl giving birth at her feet would not be seen. A girl might give birth there and leave the baby behind. Other babies, in other places, have been left behind by young girls who then walked away.

A crazy idea in a small town, of course, but if no one knew for sure she was pregnant, a young girl might persuade herself that she could get away with it.

Is that what happened?

Ask the Family. Journalists must ask the Family, after her death, what others would not ask the Family during her life.

Don't ask the State or the Church or the People. They did their duty last year, so amending the Constitution as to ensure that all pregnancies would be brought to full term. Nowhere in that amendment was provision made for life or lives beyond the point of birth.

Those are Family Matters.

Ann Lovett brought her pregnancy to full term.

On stony ground.

In winter.

Mother and child died.

Why? How?

Ask the Family.

We'll stand by them until they speak. Until they speak we'll stand by. You can't interfere with the Family, dead or alive.

Ann Lovett's sister Patricia, aged 14, died from a drug overdose on 22 April, 1984.

Nell McCafferty
February 1984

Movement, Change and Reaction
The Struggle over Reproductive Rights in Ireland

Preamble
The following article was written in November 1991, just three months before the X Case put the abortion issue right back on the centre stage of Irish politics. The details of that case and the debate surrounding it are dealt with elsewhere in this book. The struggle over women's reproductive freedom has reached a new intensity, as the implications of the 1983 anti-abortion amendment to the Irish Constitution become daily more evident and more horrific. Access to abortion information, rights to freedom of movement, bodily integrity and the unfettered provision of comprehensive reproductive health services for Irish women have once again become pivotal points in the very definition of Irish society. The experience of the opening months of 1992 confirm the extent to which the struggle over reproductive rights reflects the contradictions and the tensions at the very heart of the Irish social and cultural system.

Perhaps of all social movements in Ireland, the struggle for greater reproductive rights and fertility control has drawn on the most diverse set of strategies and tactics. Over a period of twenty years, it has utilised everything from street mobilisation to the taking of test court cases, from lobbying the legislators to direct contravention of the law. It has even undertaken the provision of services itself. The flexibility of the movement's organisational forms have undoubtedly helped it to achieve significant successes but always in the teeth of a systematic and well-organised campaign of outright opposition to every one of its demands. The intensity of debate in this area is unparalleled in recent Irish political history (other than the National Question), provoking divisions and confrontation inside a wide spectrum of social institutions, organisations and political groupings.

In this sense, the movement for choice and control over reproduction reflects well the nature of the process of social change in Irish society and the contradictory make-up of that society itself. Every aspect of reproductive control has been the subject of controversy in this state over these past two decades: contraception, sterilisation, abortion and more recently the availability of condoms as one part of a campaign for the prevention of the spread of AIDS. Ireland has had the unique experience of a referendum on fertility control in 1983, when a Constitutional amendment was carried by a 2:1 majority, providing state protection for the 'right to life of the unborn child' in all and every circumstance. As Pauline Conroy Jackson has put it:

While the amendment represented an ideological crisis for the 26-County state, it clarified many ideological problems for feminists, demonstrating clearly that control over our bodies is considered in Ireland, in 1985, to be a subversive activity. (Conroy Jackson, 1986)

Reflecting on the past twenty years, it is evident that the experience of the two decades has been very different. The 1970s was a period of offensive by the movement for reproductive rights, marked by the spectacular 'contraception train' in 1971 and closing in 1979 with the passage into law of an Act legalising, with some important restrictions, the importation and sale of contraceptives. But a powerful and well-organised reaction against the easing of access to birth control services forced the movement into retreat during the 1980s, a decade spent largely trying to defend more than to extend those precious rights. The contraception train of 1971 represents so well the experimental, enthusiastic and irreverent nature of the movement for reproductive rights in its earliest years. The Irish Women's Liberation Movement had organised this historical action by which a group of women travelled by train from Dublin to Belfast, crossed the border into Northern Ireland under British jurisdiction, and purchased condoms, contraceptive jellies, packets of the pill and spermicides to flaunt at Republic of Ireland custom officials on the return journey south. Met off the train in Dublin by chanting supporters with banners and placards, this ultimate media event ensured that women's demand for fertility control was placed firmly in the centre of Irish political life.

This simple and highly effective action brought into focus the peculiar nature of law enforcement and state authority, particularly on social issues, in Ireland. No government minister or state official displayed any interest in enforcing the letter of the law. No one in authority wished to take responsibility for jailing women for illegally importing contraceptive devices. And this was not just because of the unsympathetic glare of the media. There are many examples of situations in which governments and the state itself have opted to ignore breaches of the law rather than confront head-on the issue of reform of that law. A good example of this kind of double-think is evident at the moment in the area of marital breakdown. The absence of any state procedure to dissolve a marriage (as a result of a Constitutional prohibition on divorce) has forced couples who have had previous marriages annulled under Catholic Church procedures and who have remarried within the Catholic Church, into a position of living in 'bigamy'. Here again, the state has displayed absolute reluctance to enforce its own laws.

One result of this suspension of state authority in areas of potential social or moral conflict is a very weakened sense of the legitimacy of the state. Laws governing social and moral behaviour are expected to be broken or at least set aside when circumstances so require. For those who have devoted exhaustive energy to the task of resisting the demands for fertility control and choice, this lack of law enforcement appears to be, for the most part, acceptable. Or, at least more acceptable than the process of changing the law itself. It seems as if the legislative framework of the state is used as an 'ideal model' to which daily reality is only expected to partially conform. Many commentators have spoken of the hypocrisy which cuts through Irish society, which allows its 'representatives' to claim, for example, that there is no abortion in Ireland, despite the existence of official statistical data showing around eighty Irish women every week arriving in Britain for abortions. But it is also a feature of Irish society which causes confusion when contemporary Ireland is being analysed.

By focusing too much on the overlap between the ideology of the Catholic Church and current social laws in the Irish Republic, the conclusion is often drawn that social and private lives in this society are lived predominantly on Catholic moral lines. While there is truth in this, it misses the divergence which exists in reality (and which at times becomes a gulf) between social practices (how people live their lives) and social laws. And this dislocation is key to understanding the Irish social system.

There have been occasions, however, when the deepening contradiction between peoples' lifestyles and the law had become so overwhelming that reform of the legislation became imperative. The social movement for reproductive rights managed to exploit this contradiction to the full and eventually pushed through a law providing for limited availability of contraceptives. Many of the tactics adopted by different sections of the movement exposed both the unwillingness and inability of the state to enforce the law and also the growing numbers of women and men using birth control. Mary Robinson, currently President of the Republic, brought in a Private Members Bill with a number of other colleagues in the Senate in 1971 which, although unsuccessful, brought the issue right into the centre of the decision-making system. In the meantime Family Planning Clinics were openly providing birth control advice and selling different kinds of contraceptives. They managed to exist on the margins of the law by technically asking clients for 'donations' rather than 'payment'. Two years later, a Constitutional case (*Magee v the Attorney General*, 1973) succeeded in establishing the right of married couples to import contraceptives for their personal use, based on a clause in the Constitution ensuring the right to 'marital privacy'. In 1976, the Contraception Action Programme was launched, a campaign whose main tactic was to openly sell contraceptives using temporary retail outlets and outdoor stalls in community areas. Opinion polls regularly showed the majority of the adult population in favour of legal reform. At the same time, the number of Family Planning Clinics had increased both in Dublin and in other major cities and further attempts were being made to bring legislation through the Dáil.

One of the reasons for the ultimate success of this movement for social change was the range and variety of ways in which the battle was fought. There were, of course, heated debates and disagreements both within and between organisations. Some groups were exclusively concerned with contraception, others were interested in every aspect of fertility control. 1978 saw the emergence of the Women's Right to Choose Group, demanding free and safe contraceptive services for all and the provision of abortion. This was the first group to unambiguously demand the legalisation of abortion in Ireland, a demand on which earlier women's organisations had not reached agreement. But the movement gained strength in diversity, different sections reflecting different parts of a rapidly changing Irish society. By existing both inside and outside the parliamentary system, by exploiting every opportunity and loophole in the law, by drawing media attention to open breaches of the law, by the consistent provision of much-needed services, and by the growing strength and power of those demanding change, this was a rare example of a social movement which managed to bring about change in the rigid social structure of Irish society.

This was not a process carried out under a single organisation or within an agreed programme. Different groups and individuals made their own decisions concerning their own activities. There was no nationally coordinated campaign or movement. In fact, in most instances, there was no coordination at all. And that scarcely mattered. What did matter was that it could no longer be denied that the majority of the people wanted legal reform and that in the meantime a growing proportion of the adult population was simply taking the issue of fertility control into their own hands, backed up by the growth in semi-legal services.

But there were consequences of the slowness and unwillingness of the state to respond to the movement for change. While service provision grew, it was limited to major urban centres, linked to a mail-order service. The

Medical Card system, designed to subsidise health care for the lowest income groups, could not be used to cover the cost of contraceptives. Clinics did what they could to offset this by operating sliding scales of payment. The fact that the provision of birth control services lacked all state support meant also that its educational services were limited and its financial resources were highly restricted. Schools were not involved in birth control education and this continues to be largely the case today. The Health Service provided no facilities of any kind, and this is also predominantly true today. Only ideologically committed GPs were prepared to offer advice and medical prescriptions. Another consequence was the lack of information or real debate on the health issues associated with the use of specific forms of contraception. Access to contraception as an issue marginalised any concern with the effectiveness and possible side-effects of forms of birth control. The absence of any public services meant that those using contraceptives relied primarily on the pill, and to a lesser extent, condoms. The pill could be bought in half-yearly supplies and could be taken secretly where there was a risk of disagreement or conflict between partners.

The legalisation of contraception in 1980 did not resolve these important issues. In the first place, the law itself was highly restrictive. Contraceptives were to be available only on medical prescription. No distinction was made between condoms, spermicides or the pill itself. And contraceptives were only to be made available for 'bone fide family planning purposes' interpreted by the Minister in the Dáil (*parliament*) debate accompanying the Bill as 'married couples'. But besides making pieces of rubber available only on medical prescription, this legislation provided for *no* responsibility by the state in providing for birth control services. In many ways, the law attempted to control both the social practices and the services which had developed under conditions when contraceptives were illegal. In this it was less than successful. Family planning services continued to be provided by clinics around the country in much the same way as they had before and the restriction to 'married couples' was not adhered to in practice. Once again the law was at odds with people's lifestyles and its partial reform had not succeeded in strengthening its moral authority.

By the middle of the 1980s, some of the worst restrictions had been lifted from the law by way of an amendment to the law which went through the Dáil in 1985. The current situation is that contraceptives are available to all those over the age of eighteen years. Condoms no longer require medical prescriptions. But the Minister for Health controls the sale of contraceptives through licensing and the state has refused to date to take any further responsibility for providing comprehensive birth control services through the health or educational systems. Within the last two years Virgin Megastore has been taken to court for selling condoms at a Family Planning Clinic administered stall inside their record and clothes store. They were fined. And a further attempt to amend the law reducing the age from eighteen years to sixteen years for those wishing to avail of contraceptives has produced a minor crisis in the current Government.[1] In a related campaign, right-wing organisations have blocked attempts to include explicit references to the use of condoms in official education campaigns concerning the spread of AIDS.

But the decade of the 1980s will be remembered above every other aspect of reproductive rights for the bitter confrontation concerning the 1983 anti-abortion amendment to the Constitution. In the immediate aftermath of the introduction of contraception legislation a powerful alliance of right-wing organisations formed themselves into the Pro-Life Amendment Campaign (PLAC). While their emergence reflected a defensive reaction to the process of change which had gathered momentum during the 1970s, they quickly turned themselves into an offensive force demanding and securing commitments from the major political parties to hold a referendum on the 'right to life of the unborn child'. No social movement, other than the movement for reproductive rights, in recent Irish history, has faced such an organised, powerful and determined opposition. PLAC was made up predominantly of women, although often the spokespersons were men. It has often seemed in Ireland that where attempts are being made to hold on to the image of Irish society, despite its divergence from the actual lives of its people, it is women who play the central role. Women, who are the centre of the family, defined in the Constitution as 'the natural primary unit group of society' (*Bunreacht na hEireann*, 1937) are the standard bearers, the holders of the culture, the representatives of its soul. So, while it was women and the women's movement who had organised and demanded change in the 1970s, seeking greater control over their bodies and their lives, it was also women who formed the basis of PLAC's campaign across the country. And to what purpose? To secure a Constitutional prohibition on abortion, which was already illegal under Statute law from the nineteenth century. Perhaps the real point was to assert the power and dominance of right-wing forces after a period of change, and abortion was the easiest and safest option.

Ironically, it was the Constitution which was selected by PLAC as the instrument by which their ideological views would be imposed on the entire legal framework of the state. It was this same Constitution which had played a critical role in opening up access to contraceptives following the *Magee* case in 1973. What this reflects is the way in which the struggle for social change has time and again been diverted away from reform of statutory law towards the use of the Constitution and the courts. A parallel example can be found in the way in which the campaign for reform of the law rendering homosexuality illegal has been forced to use the European court system to achieve change. More than anything, this displacement shows just how difficult it is to win concessions from the central decision-making organ of the state, the legislature. By-passing the parliamentary process has consequences, however. It is extremely expensive to take a Constitutional case and it is also long-drawn-out and time-consuming. In addition it creates a situation whereby the population at large, as well as those directly concerned and affected, are reduced to spectators, watching experts slogging it out within the highly technical and formal atmosphere of the courts.

In the case of the abortion referendum, PLAC carried the amendment with a 2:1 majority of those who voted, and followed it up with a succession of court cases aimed at closing down pregnancy counselling services where advice and information on abortion was one of the options explored and preventing students' services from disseminating information on abortion services legally available in Britain. The pregnancy counselling services are currently challenging the ruling of the Irish courts in Europe. One consequence of the emergence of PLAC, described by Jenny Beale as 'an organised backlash against a decade of liberalisation' (Beale, 1986), was that many of those involved in the movement for reproductive rights had to establish a formal campaigning alliance in order to oppose the Constitutional amendment.

The Anti-amendment Campaign represented a new era characterised by outright confrontation, formal coordination between groups and individuals and a focus on abortion, an issue on which the reproductive rights movement had less power and much disunity. As a result, the success of PLAC's campaign saw the demoralisation and partial defeat of a movement that had achieved so much in the previous decade.

Taking a wider view of this process, there are important points to be made. PLAC was certainly highly successful but to achieve that success has also involved placing the abortion issue centrally on the political agenda in Irish society, something that would have been unimaginable a decade earlier. Questions have been raised concerning abortion under specific circumstances, for example after rape or where the woman's health is not good. And these are questions which will not go away. The debate over the amendment raged for two years, engulfing other economic and political issues. And in the referendum itself, 30 per cent of those who voted rejected the abortion amendment, while almost half the eligible electorate did not vote at all. Pointing to the underside of PLAC's victory is not intended to downplay its serious consequences. Restrictions on pregnancy advisory services are having an extremely negative effect. Clinics in England where Irish women are arriving for abortions on a daily basis have reported that they are less prepared, in many cases have not thought through the implications of their decision and are forced into circumstances of having the abortion completed immediately and returning to Ireland as if nothing has happened. The practical effect of the anti-abortion amendment has not been to reduce the number of Irish women having abortions but to ensure they are both vulnerable and isolated when implementing that decision.

And it looks like PLAC, or some similar entity, are here to stay, at least for the foreseeable future. Already some of their constituent organisations have been involved in opposing other areas of social reform. Family Solidarity has been to the forefront in opposing decriminalisation of homosexuality and that campaign is likely to gather momentum at the point at which an Irish government produces specific legislative proposals to that effect, following the favourable ruling of the European Court of Human Rights. The provision of female sterilisation services through the health system has been blocked in a number of public hospitals and sex education programmes for second level schools have also been actively, and often successfully, opposed.

So, what conclusions can be drawn on the movement for reproductive rights in Ireland? There is no doubt that it has achieved considerable change, both legal reform as well as changes in people's lifestyles. It was a movement led and made up mainly of women and its most profound impact has been on the lives of women. Irish women are exercising far greater control over their fertility than ever before. They are having fewer children and over a shorter period of their lives. The fertility rate (number of births per 1,000 women during their childbearing years) has fallen dramatically from 4.0 in 1970, to 3.3 in 1980, to 2.3 in 1987 (Blackwell, 1989). Women with children are represented to a much greater extent in formal employment and growing proportions of women are returning to work after child-rearing. Women's self-image and expectations have been transformed and although middle-class women can turn this to social and economic advantage more readily than working-class women, all women have been affected by these changes.

Women's new sense-of-themselves represents profound change in the context of Ireland's cultural tradition. Historically, attitudes to reproduction in Irish society have been bound up with our experience of famine, disease and emigration. The historical tradition of the large family has been as much a strategy for economic survival in a society with high levels of infant mortality as an ideological position drawn from Catholic thinking. Making a separation between sexual pleasure and reproduction has been an immense achievement by the movement for reproductive rights in a context where reproduction as an economic imperative has such a powerful and deep-rooted place in the collective cultural memory. Linked to this process has been the generation of a new female identity, one no longer exclusively bound up with motherhood but rather on multiple and diverse roles for current and future generations of Irish women.

The political achievements of the movement for reproductive rights have contributed much to the development of strategies by other movements for change in Irish society. The nature of the social movement for reproductive rights has altered over time as its spectacular early years gave way to longer-term organisational forms and changing attitudes. This is a pattern which has characterised the women's movement in many societies:

All social movements are constantly changing, and so is the women's movement. It seems to be general that the first period was characterised by direct, disruptive actions, great enthusiasm, intense ideological debates and organisational and personal experiments. That stage is past and has been replaced by a proliferation, fragmentation and specialisation of the movements. It has spread to ever widening circles in each country. In many countries the ideas of the movement have also reached institutions bearing some policy impact.'(Dahlerup, 1986)

The reproductive rights movement is essentially part of the women's movement and has shared its time of growth

117

and power as well as its periods of regroupment and reflection. The 1990s are likely to see the issues of abortion and decriminalisation of homosexuality appearing on the Irish political agenda. The diversity of approaches which have been a feature of the reproductive rights movement have already been drawn on by the movement for gay and lesbian rights, using the courts, service provision, lobbying and direct campaigning to maximum effect. Perhaps the experience and the impact of the struggle for reproductive rights may have created some flexibility in the Irish social system and a little bit less rigidity in the face of demands for social reform.

But the over-riding significance of the struggle for reproductive rights is that it reflects a wider confrontation over the very status of Irish women and the nature of the society we live in. Issues of fertility control have convulsed Irish society for twenety years and will continue to create intense crisis. The anti-abortion amendment inserted into the Irish Constitution radically diminishes the legal definition of woman in Irish society and puts a pregnant women into a subordinate position to that of the foetus she carries. This is an irreconcilable contradiction and one which in the long term Irish women will refuse to accept. Consequently, reproductive freedom for Irish women will continue to re-appear on the political agenda, demanding a resolution which re-establishes the full legal standing of Irish women.

Ursula Barry
November 1991

Note
1. The legislation is currently being amended to reduce the age at which contraceptives may be purchased to 17 years. *Ed, July 1992*

Outside the Jurisdiction
Irish Women Seeking Abortion

The reproductive capacities of women have long been the rationale for the allocation of distinct and separate political, economic and social roles to men and women. The struggles of women to gain control over their reproductive functions have consistently polarised debates and conflicts which surpass the narrow confines of biological reproduction into generalised discussion of the social status of women. This article attempts to argue that the issue of abortion - the induced termination of pregnancy - has served as a political terrain to curtail women's control over their reproductive functions at moments when gender divisions are under challenge from women's movements.

In the first part of the article, the historical failure of women to retain control over aspects of reproduction is examined. In a second part, some consequences of that failure for women are discussed. The tentative emergence of a women's movement and the reappearance of abortion as a public policy issue, are treated in a third part. Finally, the persistent resort to abortion abroad by Irish women is analysed in terms of the criminalisation and marginalisation of Irish women.

The Nineteenth-century Conflict

The oldest references to abortion go back to 3,000 years before Christ. There is no reference to its prohibition in the ancient Hindu, Buddhist, Greek, or pre-Moses texts. The condemnation of abortion is essentially a product of Christian philosophies, since before Christianity many societies with entirely different philosophies tolerated abortion to varying degrees and had included it in their ethics and politics (Dourlen-Rollier, 1971). In terms of historical time, absolutist legal prohibitions are quite contemporary in western countries and date back less than a century. Both English and American law in the early nineteenth century reflected a moral neutrality towards abortion which arose from a thirteenth-century belief concerning 'quickening'. This belief held that until the fourth or fifth month of pregnancy, when the foetus was capable of separate existence, it was acceptable to interfere with the course of a pregnancy (Mohr, 1978). The quickening doctrine was persistently held, pervasive and popular and adhered to by the Catholic Church, which held that the foetus became 'ensouled' at the moment of quickening. The notion of murder or moral reprobation did not arise prior to quickening.

Up to the late nineteenth century, abortion before quickening was practiced by countless women and co-existed as a form of, and alongside, primitive forms of birth control, which while not being particularly reliable were nevertheless attempted.

Abortion became a contentious contemporary issue with the rise of the movement for women's emancipation. In England, America and France abortion was a pivotal focus for the rivalry which developed between the emerging male-dominated medical corps and the female-dominated health workers, healers, midwives, wet-nurses and other female lay practitioners. The latter practised abortion as part of their repertoire of services to pregnant women.

A brief examination of this nineteenth-century opposition between male and female medical practitioners suggests that the social and legal policies which separated women health workers from women seeking services for their reproductive capacities, deprived women of access to abortion and other means to control their fertility, transferring that power over biological reproduction to male-dominated professions. In the late nineteenth-century crisis within the medical professions, one observes analogies to the contemporary debate over abortion in a country like Ireland. One notes the similar leading initiative taken by the medical élites in both instances. Abortion was projected into the political arena at moments of expansion of parallel health services. A third resemblance is that there was no evidence of a strong lobby to legalise abortion in either country at the time abortion became a public policy issue.

The 1861 Offences Against the Person Act passed in England was only one of a number of laws passed in western countries in the late nineteenth century restricting abortion and sexual behaviour. The Act deals with sexual relations between males and females, males and males, minors and adults, seducers and heiresses and animals and humans. In the reproductive sphere it criminalises abortion, attempts to procure or assist at an abortion, and regulates concealments of births.

The specific criminalisation of abortion by the British Act of 1861 was paralleled by developments in America at the time. There,

... in the 1840s and 50s, women were the backbone of the 'popular health movement'... It included many midwives and healers who regularly performed abortions ... Backed by massive amounts of philanthropic money the 'regular doctors' propagandised and lobbied to gain control over the health field ... At the same time midwifery was prohibited in most states, for the first time anywhere in the world. (CARASA, 1979)

Abortion and contraception at the time were closely associated with the emerging feminist lobby. American birth control advocate Margaret Sanger, for example, was supported by socialist women close to the American labour and syndicalist movement, such as Emma Goldmann and Elizabeth Gurley Flynn. The Labour movement to which these women addressed themselves was composed of immigrant workers, whose rates of reproduction were a source of anxiety to the political élites of the time.

In America the laws which led to the criminalising of abortion in many states were the outcome of the Physicians' Crusade Against Abortion of 1857-1880 (Noonan, 1970; Callaghan, 1970). American doctors were worried that the influx of Catholic immigrants to the USA, such as fled from Ireland after the Famine, would lead to immigrants reproducing at a faster rate than white native

Americans. Mohr (1978) in his history of abortion policy in America remarks that:

There can be little doubt that Protestant fears about not keeping up with the reproductive rates of Catholic immigrants played a greater role in the drive for anti-abortion laws than Catholic opposition to abortion did.

The Physicians' Crusade became a vehicle for the consolidation of power by the male-dominated medical profession who were locked in struggle with 'irregular' women healers, midwives and paramedics (Ehrenreich and English, 1974). By attacking the 'irregulars' who were the medical services for the mass of poor women, the crusade dealt a blow not only at women's involvement in obstetrics and gynaecology but captured for themselves a monopoly over what was to become a lucrative business with the discovery of drugs for use in labour which were sought after by more educated and wealthy women. Certainly women, too, opposed abortion but once women medical 'irregulars' were delegitimised and no longer a threat to professionalism, the issue used to obtain it - abortion - was quickly dropped. As Mohr remarks:

Regular physicians in the nineteenth century exploited the issue of abortion for a number of reasons of their own and in so doing they became the prime movers in a crucial transformation of official public policy in the Unites States. (Mohr, 1978)

The Physicians' Campaign might not have been so successful had it not been joined by other powerful institutions of the time: the law and the Press. According to Kaufmann (1984) the Campaign:

Despite its high moral tone which focused on educating the public to the dangers and evils of 'criminal abortion', the nineteenth-century anti-abortion campaign was essentially sex and class-oriented. The success of the campaign re-enforced women's sexual and social roles as mothers and specifically blocked American women's access to the information and technology of birth-control. (Kaufmann, 1984)

Midwives in England, meanwhile, had not been involved in the same popular health movement as in the USA, but the same rivalry surfaced. While obstetrics was recognised as a speciality in 1858, male doctors were not actually required to train for confinements until decades later. It was not until 1888 that attendance at a minimum of twelve births was a requirement for qualification in the speciality (Jennings, 1982). The English midwives tried to organise themselves to upgrade their status as the power of doctors grew. They tried to integrate into the medical profession but this was fiercely resisted by the doctors. The midwives' attempts to raise their working standards was seen by some of them as a political campaign for women's rights. One prominent midwife of the period describes it:

For nearly twenty years before the passing of the Midwives Act in 1902 a small band of devoted women laboured in season and out of season urging on Parliament the need of a Bill requiring a minimum of three months theoretical and practical training and examination before trusting a woman with the lives of mother and child. This historical fact alone is sufficiently cogent reason for the now ever increasing demand on the part of women for the Parliamentary vote ... (Morley, 1914)

In contrast to their American counterparts, English midwives sought to professionalise themselves as a paramedical institution, yet despite legal prohibitions on abortion dating back forty years, had failed to do so by the turn of the century.

The English and American midwives were not alone in finding themselves threatened with exclusion from the care of women's reproduction. In Paris the nineteenth century midwives found themselves locked in a rivalry with the doctors in which abortion was to play a crucial part. By 1892, the French medical profession had obtained a legal monopoly on obstetrical, gynaecological and medical acts including exclusive right to use the forceps in delivery. In terms of scientific discovery, the forceps was an easily diffusable item at popular level, requiring no capital outlay for its use. Apart from the legal constraints on women practitioners midwives were repeatedly attacked in the French press:

If these attacks were constant, their form varied with time. First their arrogance and ignorance were branded, then from 1880 on they were accused of spreading puerperal fever and by the turn of the century, the theme of midwife-abortionist was developed continuously until World War I. (Tucat, 1971)

The gradual exclusion of midwives from legal access to

pregnant mothers debarred women from not only the possibility of an abortion but also from the practice of contraception which many doctors opposed.

For those women who chose to pioneer entry to the medical profession to become doctors, the path was no clearer. Just prior to the passing of the 1861 Offences Against the Person Act, Miss Elizabeth Blackwell applied in 1858 to have her name placed on the General Medical Council list of practitioners. She succeeded. Miss Garrett Anderson - a newly qualified doctor - followed suit in 1865. But following the success of these women, medical schools changed their rules and prohibited women from following medical training. It took the establishment of an all-female medical unit for women to break into the profession in England (Jordanova, 1984; L'Espérance, 1977).

As for the alleged benefits that the switch from female to male profession was supposed to bring, this was not immediately apparent. The expected fall in infant and maternal mortality rates did not occur. The death of thousands of women from puerperal fever continued into the twentieth century. Schrom Dye observes that although antisepsis had been discovered in the 1840s, it was not widely practiced until well into the twentieth century:

Although midwives were usually blamed for the high death rate in the first two decades of the [twentieth] century, mortality rates increased after midwives had been all but eliminated as birth attendants ... many American doctors were unconvinced by or ignorant of the importance of antisepsis - a practice that did not become routine in American hospitals until the end of the nineteenth century. (Schrom Dye, 1980; Ehrenreich and English, 1974)

The accusation that midwives caused puerperal fever was a frightening spectre to raise. In Ireland, for example, the delirium which appeared at the height of puerperal fever was often misdiagnosed and was frequently taken to be puerperal mania and thus reason for committal to an asylum (Finnane, 1981). There the women, in an already weak state of health, frequently died. The 1861 Act was the outcome of a struggle which was under way in those countries where a male-dominated medical profession was trying to prevent women having access to other women for the purposes of health and care in their reproductive lives. In England, the USA and France, the medical males gained the upper hand, not through force of argument, not through the efficacy of their methods but by political control over the legislatures which endowed them with exclusive monopoly over women's reproductive functions.

The Catholic Church was rather tardy in responding to the rise of the women's movements, the increasing use of abortion and the new scientific discoveries about contraception and fertilisation. It was not until 1869, considerably after the commencement of the debate on abortion, that Pius IX dropped any reference to 'ensouled foetus' in the excommunication for abortion. Even then not all theologians agreed with him. Indeed, the principal draftsman of *Casti Connubii* - the papal encyclical which deals with marriage, family and contraception - maintained that there was little solid evidence for immediate diffusion of the soul at conception, which implied that prior to then, abortion might be justified. It was not until 1917 that the abortion excommunication was extended to the pregnant mother, who hitherto had been excluded. The Catholic Church was in this sense a moral follower and not a leader in patriarchal trends.

The end of the nineteenth century saw the separation of women healers from those who had previously sought their services as abortionists. This separation was accomplished by legal and political restrictions on the practice of medicine by women. The regularising of medicine deregularised abortion and drove it underground into clandestinity where it has lurked well into the late twentieth century when the rise of women's movements and new crises in the medical profession transformed it into a crucial theme in the transformation of women's subordinated position in society.

Twentieth century Judicial and Legal Interventions
The consequences of the defeat of the women's movement in the area of reproductive policies is visible in the 20th century judicial and legal enforcement of control over

women's reproduction. The period of 1930-1950 illustrates this.

In 1935 a Bill to criminalise contraception was placed before the Dáil (*parliament*) - a Bill which was the outcome of an all-party committee on sexual and reproductive matters. The official description of the Criminal Law Amendment Bill gives little clue to its contents; this was an Act: *For the protection and suppression of brothels and prostitution and for those and other purposes to amend the law relating to sexual offences.* It was section 17 of the Bill which prohibited the sale, advertising and importing for sale of contraceptives. Contraception had been effectively legal for fifteen years up to this point. A solitary voice expressed objections to section 17 at Committee stage. Dr Rowlette TD warned that the section would lead to an increase in criminal infanticide and criminal abortion (Dáil Reports: 1935 A). The Bill illustrates the legislators' close linking of measures for the control of fertility with prostitution. Indeed, the monetary penalties for using contraceptives were twenty-five times greater than those for prostitution, reflecting an assumption that controlling one's reproductive capacities was more grievous than controlling the sale of one's body.

Opposing section 17, Deputy Rowlette had referred to infanticide and abortion. The increase in infanticide is to an extent supported by the remarks of a presiding judge reported in the *Cork Examiner* of 1929 as follows (Rose, 1976):

His lordship, referring to cases of concealment of birth, said the number of newly-born infants in the country who were murdered by their mother at present surpassed belief. Only one out of fifty came up in the courts, but there was a wholesale slaughter of these innocents going on through the country.

In contrast to the paucity of comment on sexuality and reproduction, a raging debate was taking place in the Dáil at the same time on the position of women in the manufacturing workforce. This was happening during the debate on the Conditions of Employment Bill, presented to the Dáil by Seán Lemass. He described that Bill as having the purpose of:

Making regulations preventing the employment of women on any class of work on which it is undesirable that women should be engaged (Dáil Reports, 1935 B).

Lemass expressed the opinion that:

I think most deputies will agree that it would create social problems of the first magnitude if there should be any considerable acceleration of the tendency to replace men by women in industrial work (Dáil Reports, 1935 C). I am aware that there has been a certain opposition to this section of the Bill on the ground that ... it is retrogressive of an anti-feminist nature. (Dáil Reports, 1935 D)

Debate on the two Bills to control women's place in industrial production and biological reproduction alternated during the Dáil session of the period, demonstrating a remarkable consistency on the legislature's part in their perception of the interlocking relationship between the two spheres. These two pieces of legislation criminalised women's attempts to use birth control to enter certain paid employments in industrial work.

By the time the two Bills had passed, eleven prosecutions or investigations into illegal backstreet abortions had already been undertaken by the Gardaí (*police*) (Rose, 1976). Meanwhile in England the acquittal of Dr Alec Bourne following his prosecution for the offence of terminating the pregnancy of a thirteen-year-old girl, gang-raped by soldiers, had liberalised interpretations of the 1861 Offences Against the Person Act. Following the Bourne judgement, prosecutions for illegal abortions in the 26 Counties of Ireland dropped quickly. From this we may surmise that the so-called abortion trail to England started not in 1967 but some thirty years earlier, about 1937.

The respite for Irish women seeking abortion was shortlived. With the outbreak of World War II, restrictions on travel to England were introduced, with the exception of professionals, those going on business and seasonal workers (defined as males). Women were temporarily replacing men in British industry and there may have been fears that Irish women emigrants would flood the labour market and depress wages and conditions. To the extent that that is the case, restrictions on women's place in production (in England) had immediate consequences for Irish women seeking abortions (in England). Prosecutions for backstreet abortions soared in Ireland to a new peak. Between 1942 and 1946 the number of investigations and prosecutions reached twenty-five recorded cases (Rose, 1976).

Judge Davitt at the end of a trial of an electrician-cum-instrument maker with no medical qualifications whatsoever, who charged £120 for a backstreet abortion, commented: 'It is a melancholy reflection that for the past few weeks I have been trying these cases and nothing else' (*The Irish Times*, 1944).

Not only did backstreet abortion increase, so did the illegitimacy rate. By 1945, illegitimate births as a percentage of live births reached 3.93 per cent - the highest proportion ever recorded between 1864 and 1977. With the ending of travel restrictions, both abortion investigations and illegitimate births fell.

That policy-makers knew the consequences of absolute control over women's reproduction is clear from the Reports of the Commission on Emigration and Other Population Problems which sat between 1948 and 1954. Attention is given in their reports to population control, birth control and family planning - all of which were equally deplored. Noting that the rate of infant mortality among illegitimate children was 73 per cent higher than for legitimate children, the Commission commented that:

While adequate information is lacking as to the extent of infanticide, we believe that the incidence is not sufficiently significant to require comment from us. (Commission on Emigration Reports, 1954)

Comment there was from the Press of the period. While the commission was in session, a Mrs X was sentenced to fifty-six years in prison for procuring abortions on eight women for approximately 20 shillings per woman. Two years after the commission finished its work, the body of Mrs Y, mother of six children, was found lying dead, on the footpath at Hume Street, Dublin. A major trial followed of a woman accused of murdering her in the course of a backstreet abortion. The accused was tried and sentenced to death, a sentence later commuted to life imprisonment. The accused died in prison (*The Irish Times*, 1956).

The fragments of evidence presented here, for the period 1930-1950, suggest that neither the mysterious death rate of illegitimate infants, the incidence of backstreet abortion nor the risk and actual deaths of women who might resort to such clandestine operations convinced policy-makers of the need to shift one centimetre from a policy of absolute control over reproduction. The inability of the women's groups and associations of the period to rally women to redress some of the injustices they experienced left the legislature and judiciary intact in their patriarchal mode of thought. This, notwithstanding the bravery of members of the Irish Women's Workers Union in breaching the war-time embargo on strikes by marching laundry workers to Government Buildings to seek better working hours. It was not until the late 1960s, when women's groups and associations formed, demanding a whole range of radical and moderate reforms, that the absolutism of the control over women's reproduction was somewhat eroded.

Reappropriating Control

In the late 1960s, women's groups emerged and formed in European and North American regions. Similarly to what had happened a century earlier, they included women of different social classes and interests and took issue with women's lack of control over their reproduction and their unequal place in and out of the workforce. In Dublin women formed a convoy to illegally import and display contraceptives bought in the North. In 1969 a Fertility Guidance Clinic opened in Dublin and a year later a Family Planning Rights Group formed. Illegal family planning clinics and abortion referral centres followed, in particular after the passing of the 1967 Abortion Act in England. The Women's Liberation Group, Irish Women United and other radical groups included in their demands changes in women's control over work and their reproductive capacities. Rape Crisis Centres, Women's Aid Hostels and publishing collectives of women opened up North and South, creating a parallel network of services which were particularly strong in the health arena. Abortion, however, remained a taboo subject in most women's groups and few dared to articulate demands that it be included among the 'rights' that ought to be reappropriated by women. By 1980, just one solitary and brief pamphlet had been published on the subject by a women's group. The deafening silence on the subject of abortion suggests that its criminalisation was so internalised as to constitute an obstacle to even learned and academic investigation of the subject, with some notable exceptions (Walsh, 1976). Without discussion, abortion as a subject lacked a public language or vocabulary for its contextualisation and conceptualisation. Paradoxically it was not until a proposal emerged to amend the Constitution in relation to abortion that any form of public language appeared with which to conceptualise abortion.

Irish Women Seek Abortions

The number of Irish women recorded as seeking abortions in England has been rising in the 26 Counties and remaining static in the Six Counties since 1967. Five studies of women using abortion or contraception referral services show consistency in the social characteristics of women seeking abortion (Irish Pregnancy Counselling Service, 1979; Burke, 1983; Walsh, 1975; Ulster Pregnancy Advisory Service, 1984; Dean, 1984). In terms of age women in the 20-29 age group comprise the largest number of women concerned. The number of teenagers seeking abortion is greater in the Six than in the 26 Counties. In the 26 Counties studies, 13-14 per cent of women were married and these proportions showed no change over the decade. The numbers describing themselves as divorced or separated did seem to rise. The proportion married in the Six Counties was notably higher than in the 26 Counties. Contrary to media stereotyping, unmarried teenage girls are not seeking abortion for unwanted or accidental pregnancies. This is not borne out by research. Indeed the age group and geographical predominance of urban origins among women seeking abortions in England, suggests that it is young urban women who use the 1967

Abortion Act in England, while their teenage counterparts tend to proceed with their pregnancies (Dean, 1984).

Excluding miscarriage and abortion, between 25 per cent and 33 per cent of women seeking abortion have already given birth to a child. The study by Sandra Burke for Open Door went into more detail and ascertained that the 48 mothers seeking their referral service had some 131 children between them, the equivalent of a three-teacher National School!

Among women seeking abortion the numbers reporting that they had previously had a pregnancy terminated seem to rise sharply in the early 1980s; tripling from 3 per cent in 1980 to 10-11 per cent in 1983 (Burke, 1983; Dean, 1984). This may arise from different methods of enquiry or reflect an increase in the use of abortion as a form of birth control.

This brings us to the issue of contraception. The numbers reporting that they had not used contraception, while lower in the Six than the 26 Counties, is still remarkably high, ranging from 31 per cent to 42 per cent of women seeking abortions.

It is of interest that the Open Door study was carried out with the cooperation of women seeking abortion during the campaign on the Eighth Amendment to the 1937 Constitution in the weeks before and after actual voting. Some 200 women sought their services during this period. The campaign may have presented 'abortion' as an option to women who might not have previously contemplated it.

As for the question of why individual women seek abortions - this is most difficult to study. Two studies - Well Woman and Open Door - asked women questions related to this issue. In both instances only 4 per cent gave health as a reason. Among Well Woman service users, 45 per cent of women said that they could not face their parents or could not cope with a pregnancy. Other reasons cited by Open Door users were fear of pregnancy among older women, marital breakdown, large families and fear of job loss.

In contrast to the low proportions citing health as a reason for seeking abortion, Walsh (1975) reports that 88 per cent of Irish women seeking a pregnancy termination under the 1967 Abortion Act in England in 1971/72 did so on the grounds of mental or psychiatric disorder. Since the physical or mental health of the mother is one of the main grounds for termination of pregnancy in England, one deduces from this discrepancy in cited reasons that women seeking abortions in England present their situation in terms of a mental health disorder. Irish women seeking abortion in England are not merely criminalised but apparently must present themselves as mentally disturbed to successfully obtain an abortion.

Examining the rise in the numbers of women from the 26 Counties seeking abortion, one observes a shift in the popularity of options other than abortion, such as adoption. Over the decade of the 1970s, the popularity of adoption fell. The decline in the popularity of adoption among unmarried mothers suggests that more and more pregnant unmarried mothers are deciding to give birth and rear their children themselves. This does not however appear to be the case when one compares the ratio of abortion to illegitimate births among single women.

In Table 1 the ratio of illegitimate births to abortions among single women is estimated for the period 1971-1984. The ratio is derived from a comparison of the numbers of illegitimate births in the 26 Counties with the numbers of abortions carried out in England on Irish women residents of the 26 Counties. In 1971, for every one abortion in England among unmarried women, there were three illegitimate births in Ireland. By the end of the decade, for almost every abortion there was one illegitimate birth in Ireland. So, looking at adoption figures alone suggests that the status of unmarried mothers is becoming popular. Comparing the numbers of pregnancies and terminations among unmarried women suggests that unmarried mother and pregnancy termination are now equally popular. Indeed for some age groups of single women in their twenties, abortion is already a more popular option than continuing with the pregnancy.

The campaign to insert the amendment into the Irish

Constitution in 1983 which had the effect of prohibiting the legislature from enacting a law to legalise abortion without a further referendum, did not take place against a backdrop of demands by women's groups to legalise abortion. Indeed at the time of the amendment the reported numbers of women from Northern Ireland having pregnancies terminated in England was actually falling (see Table 2), indicating some volatility in the use of abortion for Ireland as a whole. It did occur at a time of demand for improved social legislation in the field of maternity leave, illegitimacy, divorce, contraception, and married women's domicile. As with the nineteenth-century

Table 1. Estimated Numbers of Pregnancies Terminated on Single Women Compared with Numbers of Unmarried Mothers in 26 Counties, 1971-84.

Year	Terminations on Single Irish Women in UK	Illegitimate Births in 26 Counties	Ratio of Columns (2) + (3)
(1)	(2)	(3)	
1971	625	1842	2.9
1973	955	2167	2.2
1974	1137	2309	2.0
1975	1259	2515	1.9
1976	1457	2545	1.7
1977	1748	2879	1.6
1978	2039	3003	1.4
1979	2244	3337	1.4
1980	2656	3691	1.3
1981	2916	3911	1.3
1982	2923	4351	1.5
1983	2938	4517	1.5
1984	*3170	*5012	

Sources: Office of Population Censuses and Surveys. Govt. Statistical Service. Abortion Statistics UK. Report on Vital Statistics compiled by CSO, Dublin, 1983. Quarterly Report on Birth, Deaths and Marriages and Infectious Diseases 1983, Dept. of Health, Dublin, July 1984.

* = estimate based on the first two quarters of year.

anti-abortion campaigns, the coalition of forces supporting the Constitutional amendment held strong views on the retention of laws and values which see women as primarily home-based mothers, sexually and socially subordinate to men. The established medical élite played a leading role in initiating and sustaining the pro-amendment campaign, as their American, French and British counterparts had done a century earlier. Their lobbying was not intended to offer alternatives to women who seek abortion, but to block legislative enactments which might, at some time in the future, endorse the medical termination of pregnancies. Since the passage of the amendment, there have been several cases of infanticide and/or birth concealment, mainly in rural areas. These occurrences tend to give sustenance to the thesis argued by Rose (1976) and O'Connor (1985) that infanticide was a preferred option for dealing with unwanted pregnancy in nineteenth-century Ireland. If this was the case, these contemporary events are not isolated exceptions but the continuance, albeit on a minor scale, of historical patterns of response to unwanted pregnancy.

Table 2: number of Pregnancy Terminations in England to Women from Northern Ireland.

Year	Number of Terminations
1974	1092
1975	1115
1976	1142
1977	1244
1978	1311
1979	1425
1980	1565
1981	1441
1982	1510
1983	1460

Source: Office of Population Censuses and Surveys, Government Statistical Service. Abortion Statistics, UK.

Conclusions

The separation of female medical workers from their female clients in the late nineteenth century by the professionalisation of medicine, the outlawing and subordination of midwifery, and legal monopolies on new obstetric technology deprived women of an access to abortion to which they had become accustomed. Abortion was used in the nineteenth century as a vehicle for the exclusion of women from the caring professions and from exercising control over reproduction, gynaecology and obstetrics. The positions developed by the Catholic Church followed rather than preceded these secular developments and constituted a retrospective legitimation of patriarchy in relation to women's reproduction and sexuality, both of which were sacrificially fused into one. This sacrifice was at the expense of the development of policies to provide women with any measure of reproductive freedom: to have as well as not to have the children they and their partners chose. The sacrifice had a cost. The cost is the gynocidal (Daly, 1978) policies towards women's reproductive functions in Ireland. Gynocidal in the sense of mutilation, deformation and exhaustion of the reproductive capacities of women. These have taken the form of attempts at self-induced abortion (Burke, 1983), illegal and horrific backstreet abortion, offering to women seeking sterilisation the sole option of womb removal, the medical validation of repeated caesarian deliveries, the use here as elsewhere of the now discredited automatic breast removal operations for cancer, the introduction of laws specifying the amount of radiation pregnant working women may be exposed to, not to mention the offering of massive doses of hormonal drugs in contraception, menopause, morning-after pills and miscarriage prevention.

Abortion, it has been argued, has been used as a fertile terrain for contesting changes in women's rights to control their reproductive capacities, thereby disassociating sexuality and reproduction, at moments of crisis in the gender division of labour. This appears to have been the case in the US, France and England in the nineteenth

135

century. In Ireland in the 1930s, it seems to have been the case when laws were enacted almost simultaneously regulating women's place in production and reproduction. Public policy on abortion was an issue in the 1984 USA Presidential Elections at the moment that a woman was nominated vice-presidential Democratic candidate.

The extension of property relations to the contents of the womb, consequent on the passage of the Eighth Amendment to the Constitution, has no equivalent male counterpart. It is not unique to Ireland. The same extension of property relations to the wombs of Chinese women (Chan Shutting, 1983) is leading to socially compulsory abortion and the re-emergence in China of infanticide and a reversal of the western meaning of the slogan: 'the right to choose'. The close connection of property relations, population control and women's reproduction is evident in the encouragements to Irish travelling women to accept birth control, sterilisation and even the infamous injectible contraceptive Depo Provera (*Evening Press*, 1983), encouragements notably lacking when one treats of the settled population of women. Internal to the treatment of women's reproduction are profound social class cleavages. Class-differentiated treatments of women's reproduction permeates gynaecology, obstetrics and medical care right through the type of contraception proposed as acceptable to working-class women. The Intra-uterine Device (IUD) for example seems more popular (or promoted?) among working-class than middle-class women, according to one reported study of users (Dáil Reports, 1983). As a form of contraception it requires less reflection and education in its use, compared to the Pill, or Diaphragm, which require conscious and continuous decision-making; qualities which may be presumed lacking or unnecessary in working-class women.

It is in the context of global population control and compulsory reproductive controls especially on working class and minority women that the 'choice' of abortion is being re-examined critically by many feminist writers (Rich, 1977) who would rank abortion along with other gynocidal practices as an increasingly reluctant and involuntary option chosen by women in the absence of the means to safely control their fertility and in the void of environmental and social opportunities to exercise an authentic reproductive freedom.

As gender divisions come under increasing scrutiny and increasing numbers of women elect to risk criminalising themselves by providing and availing of counselling services and later proceeding with abortions in England, it is highly unlikely that abortion will fade out as a policy issue, though its suitability as a vehicle for contesting women's rights in general has probably been temporarily exhausted in the 26 Counties. In the Six Counties, the opening of a campaign to have the 1967 British Abortion Act extended to Northern Ireland, would, if successful, catapult the abortion issue back into the 26 Counties and furnish women with a much cheaper and more accessible form of usage of the 1967 Act.

Pauline Conroy Jackson
1987

The Politics of Abortion in a Police State

Living in a Police State

Police state: State regulated by means of a national police having supervision and control of the activities of citizens. *Police*: existing for the regulation, discipline and control of the community. *(Oxford English Dictionary)*

Women in Ireland are living in a police state. The term is not one to be bandied about in the Irish context and I do not use it lightly now. I mean, quite plainly, that the reproductive activities of women in Ireland are being subjected to a process of 'regulation, discipline and control', carried out by the police in accordance with state policy and laws. The policing of women's reproduction was implicitly sanctioned by the Eighth Amendment to the Constitution and explicitly empowered by the High Court ruling on information in 1986, and by the rulings of the Supreme Court in 1988. If Protocol Number 17 remains appended to the Maastricht Treaty and if this treaty is ratified, the control zone will be liable to further extension.

Over the past several months the policing of women has accelerated at an unprecedented rate. During this time, the state, in the form of the legislature, has abdicated its legislative function by refraining from drafting legislation on the issue of abortion despite being reminded of its responsibility to do so by the Supreme Court in its ruling in the X case. The Government has adopted a strategy of postponement and evasion, apparently operating on the principle that 'time solves all problems'. Which of course it does not, least of all in the case of pregnancy. Women continue - literally - to bear the brunt of legislative inertia and cowardice because the Gardaí *(police)* have no option but to 'police' reproducing women since this is what is required if the 'law' is to be enforced.

The interpretation of the law, in so far as it exists at all, is unclear in the extreme: one information case is currently before the European Commission of Human Rights, while another is before the European Court of Justice. The law is also largely unenforceable: approximately eighty women continue to obtain pregnancy terminations in Britain every week. Not even the most diligent of police forces could consistently 'supervise and control' the reproductive practices and intentions of approximately one million women of child-bearing age in this country. The flow of information to women who need it has indeed been seriously interfered with - but not entirely staunched, no more than the flow of Irish women across the water.

The police are therefore reduced to using the tactics of guerilla warfare, taking sporadic and wild swipes at the more visible 'transgressors' of the law. The 'law-breakers' are invariably vulnerable individuals and organisations, such as Open Line Counselling and the student unions. They are not rich, they are not powerful and precisely because they expose and succeed in circumventing the hypocrisy, absurdity and cruelty of unworkable laws, these individuals and organisations do not enjoy the protection of the state and its institutions.

Given the inadequacy of the law, the information base on which the Gardaí must take action is at best uncertain and sometimes downright wrong; it is in any case heavily dependent on informants who choose to 'assist' the Gardaí by informing them of infringements or of *possible* infringements, of the law. It is the well-orchestrated and well-tried practice of certain extreme right-wing groups to alert the Gardaí, in advance, to the possibility of an offence being committed. The promptness with which the agents of the state jump to attention is a disturbing facet of this supposedly democratic society. Who, we must ask, really pulls the state strings? Who masterminds the political agenda?

It is obvious that in the politically hyper-sensitive and legally ambiguous minefield of abortion regulation in this country, the margin for error is wide, which does nothing to enhance the credibility of the Gardaí. The targets of their guerilla-type forays are thus often ludicrous - such as the attempt to prevent a woman from importing from Belfast, for non-commercial use, copies of *The Guardian* newspaper containing an advertisement for the Marie Stopes clinic. But as we know from the X case, these forays can also be life-threatening. Such tactics veer from the insane, to the inane, to the dangerous. Not all derive directly from police intervention -- some are the consequence of self-censorship in a climate where the fear of reprisals, in the form of injunctions or arrests, is based on a realistic assessment of precedent.

Over the past six months and more we have witnessed or experienced:

(a) direct and indirect censorship:

• through the continuing ban preventing health clinics and services from providing information about abortion services abroad.

• through the continuing ban on the publication of information about abortion services abroad by student unions and, by extension, by any other publisher.

• through the removal by the public library system of health manuals, including the highly respected *Our Bodies Our Selves* (published in the UK by Penguin Books), from the shelves of public libraries in Dublin. The books were removed (although later replaced) because they contained names and addresses of clinics carrying out abortions in Britain.

• through serious threats by members of Dublin Corporation that London telephone directories would be removed from Dublin libraries because they contain names and addresses of clinics carrying out abortions in Britain.

• through the banning of the sale in Ireland of an American anti-abortion organising manual because it contained names and addresses of abortion clinics in the USA. Ironically, the clinics were listed as targets for the anti-abortion movement while the Irish booksellers banned from selling the book are an important publishing outlet of the Catholic Church.

• through the decision of the Irish distributors not to distribute for sale copies of *The Guardian* newspaper carrying an advertisement by the Marie Stopes clinic. While the Gardaí did not directly intervene in this case, they were present at the airport when the distributors made their decision. The distributors feared, of course, that they would be subjected to judicial injunction, based on precedents in previous 'information' cases.

• through the continuous low-level harassment of a feminist publishing house in the form of complaints by anonymous individuals to advertisers, distributors and booksellers, concerning the 'moral unacceptability' of its publications and resulting in certain cases in their necessary withdrawal from circulation.

• through the refusal of a radio station to broadcast a live interview with representatives of the British-based Marie Stopes organisation on the basis that such an interview might be against the law. This should be placed in the context of the earlier RTE ban on any live discussion of the 'abortion issue' for the same reasons.

(b) police and judicial intervention

• the recall to Ireland by the Gardaí of a fourteen-year-old girl and her parents who had travelled to the UK for an abortion following the fourteen-year-old's rape-induced pregnancy (the X case). The High Court granted an interim injunction against the girl and her parents, which it later confirmed, although this was subsequently overturned by the Supreme Court. The Supreme Court ruled that in the event of 'real and substantial risk' (which it did not define) to the life of the pregnant woman, she would be entitled to seek legal abortion in Ireland.

• in the X case, the Supreme Court did not, however, establish the right of women in Ireland (of whatever nationality) to travel abroad to obtain abortion. Technically, women can be interned inside the state if there are grounds to suspect they may leave the state for the purposes of availing of abortion services - services which are legally available to all other EC citizens.

• Protocol Number 17 was appended to the Maastricht Treaty at the request of the Irish Government with the aim of removing the issue of abortion in Ireland from the ambit of EC policy and law. Although the precise meaning and effect of this Protocol are now disputed by lawyers, the clear political intention of its insertion was to ensure that women in Ireland would not be entitled to any increase in their rights with regard to abortion as a consequence of Ireland's participation in the European Union.

• the questioning and brief arrest of an Irish woman who had sought to import twenty copies, for non-commercial purposes, of the effectively censored 'Marie Stopes' issue of *The Guardian*.

• the arrival of the Gardaí at the premises of a local radio station when informed that the station intended to broadcast the text of the Marie Stopes *Guardian* advertisement. It was promptly pointed out to the Gardaí that this would not be illegal since the text of the advertisement had been read into the Dáil (*Parliament*) record by Democratic Left TD, Proinsias De Rossa, and subsequently published and broadcast by the national media as the perfectly legal record of Dáil proceedings.

• the Gardaí reportedly investigated reports of this very meeting here in Cork on the basis that the meeting would 'give information about abortion'. Whether the Gardaí actually did investigate the legality of the meeting is not the most important point. *Reports* that the Gardaí were doing so were of themselves sufficient to dissuade women from attending. And that is a totally unacceptable situation in a democratic state where the right to free assembly is being jeopardised.

There are, no doubt, other incidents that I am unaware of. I do know that countless women, including myself and others whom I know well, have been subjected to unpleasant and frightening personal and professional harassment by extreme right-wing organisations and individuals, many of them very powerfully placed indeed. I am absolutely certain that very many Irish women postponed or cancelled their plans to seek termination of pregnancy in the UK or travelled to Britain in fear and uncertainty, not knowing what actions might be taken against them on their return. These incidents are not the fault of the Gardaí. They are a consequence of the contorted and contradictory position adopted by the Government, whereby it persists in its aim of controlling women's reproduction but refrains from drafting measures which would enable it to do so with, at the very least, a degree of clarity. But the Government has its own agenda and women's freedom is definitely not on it.

Censorship and police and judicial intervention, combined with confused and confusing laws and governmental evasion, greatly exacerbate the climate of difficulty and fear in which Irish women must live their sexual and reproductive lives. Numerous aspects of sexuality and sexual behaviour are literally unspeakable because never spoken of. Abortion as personal experience is a taboo topic. Abortion may be discussed only within the context of moral, legal and political debate. Abortion is represented as either moral or immoral, legal or illegal, permissible or prohibited: the fact that it is a personal and material experience, a social, economic and psychological necessity cannot be referred to without fear of sanction in our 'policed' culture. A woman may not easily declare in public, or indeed in private, that she has had an abortion. A woman may not even easily declare that she is pro-choice.

The absolute stigma once attached to single motherhood (which lingers, if the truth be told, with considerable tenacity), has been transferred or extended to abortion. Some argue that this is progress: I read it as the ability of the state and its institutions to consistently thwart women's fight for reproductive freedom. I read it as a sign that we are engaged in a continuing struggle where victory is never absolute and opponents must never be trusted.

In a general sense, the question of 'reproductive freedom' for women in Ireland is highly problematic. It is still the case that womanhood and motherhood are represented as synonymous realities, as the latest statement from the Catholic hierarchy makes abundantly clear:

This teaching in no way implies that the life of the unborn child is 'preferred' to the life of the mother, or that the mother's life is to be 'sacrificed' to save the child. Both lives are equally precious. The life of the pregnant mother is as inviolable as is the life of the child in her womb. (*The Irish Times*, 27 May 1992)

143

Quite apart from the extraordinary - and unsuccessful - convolutions of the bishops' attempt to engineer a 'balance of rights', their repeated use of the word 'mother' when 'woman' is the technically accurate term must be read as the rhetorical tool of a highly manipulative discourse - pregnant women are not necessarily 'mothers' and may not, for all kinds of reasons, become 'mothers'. But for the bishops, only mothers are 'real women' - and 'real women' are not sexual: 'womanhood' is symbolically and materially non-existent until non-sexually osmosed into 'motherhood':

We turn to Mary, the New Eve, Mother of all the living and ask for her motherly intercession. At the message of the Angel, the Word became flesh in Mary's womb through the overshadowing of the Holy Spirit.(*The Irish Times*, 27 May 1992)

So who believes the bishops? The evidence of the opinion polls taken in the months since the X case and its public aftermath show a growing recognition and acceptance of the social need for abortion in limited circumstances, irrespective of Catholic moral teaching. And there can be no doubt that the moral authority of the hierarchy has been undermined by the recent exposure of Bishop Casey as a 'secret' father. The numbers of the faithful now reading the bishops' homilies with a (privately) raised eyebrow and a large grain of salt must indeed be on the increase. Nonetheless, an opinion poll is not a vote and it would be flying in the face of Irish social history in the twentieth century to underestimate - far less to write off - the power of Catholic discourse to shape social and political practices.

In a society where motherhood remains virtually the only secure source of canonised validation for the vast majority of women, the decision *not* to be a mother is deeply subversive and risky. The traditional social pressures on women to reproduce (several times) remain strong, vehicled through Roman Catholic ideology operating within the education and health systems, the law, the political arena, the family as an institution and the labour force. Children and young people do not generally benefit from sex education at school, and investment in reproductive education for girls and women is virtually nil. Contraceptives are available in principle, by law, in pharmacies throughout the country - in practice, this is often not the case, with women frequently too intimidated to ask for them in small rural communities.

There is a marked class dimension to women's access to reproductive health services: money, and location in some instances, can buy you a different doctor, a different pharmacy, travel to a Family Planning or Well Woman centre, travel to Britain for an abortion without the risk of incurring debt or job loss. These are important differences which are never recognised by either our political or moral arbiters. The right to travel is of no bodily use to women who have no money to travel. But neither money nor class position can buy relief from the fear of exposure and stigmatisation. Money does not buy freedom from fear.

The policing of women's reproductive functions in Ireland cannot and will not cease until such time as the legislature, our elected representatives, are willing and able to recognise that reproduction is a social process, not a legal matter or a moral issue; that women are social and moral agents, capable of making reasoned and responsible decisions and with the right to do so in a democracy. The policing of women cannot and will not cease until such time as the legislature and all other institutions of the state have the courage to resist coercion by powerful and extreme right-wing forces which seek to impose their version of morality on the population as a whole.

The Politics of Abortion
Abortion politics are unrelenting, brutal and brutalising. While the situation is particularly vicious in Ireland at present, the onslaught on women's freedom is an inter-national phenomenon, with a long history and powerful tentacles into both neo-fascism and fundamentalism.

The politics of abortion is not about Maastricht any more than it is about morality. It is about power. Specifically, it is about the exercise of male power. It is about men's obsession with ownership and control of 'their' seed, not one precious drop of which must be wasted. It is about their overriding desire for dominance

145

and their identification of reproduction as a primary site for the control of women. Abortion is crucially about male ownership of women.

Sociologist Anne Oakely points out that the management and control of reproduction are 'inseparable from how women are managed and controlled'. Abortion is never just about 'abortion' and women cannot afford to think that it is. We need to see the 'abortion issue' (which happens to be a concrete experience for countless thousands of Irish women) in the broad context of reproductive freedom and in the even broader context of women's historical struggle for social and political self-hood.

Reproductive freedom has been a central issue for feminism and the Women's Movement since the nineteenth century because reproduction has been - is - a central part of women's lives and the arena in which male control has been consistently exercised. In the White West, the struggle has focused on birth control, abortion, and more recently on the development of reproductive technologies. For Black women in the West, for women elsewhere in the world, the struggle has often centred around other reproductive issues - notably around population control strategies such as enforced sterilisation and limitation of family size.

Depending on class, race, ethnic origin, global location, it can seem as if women are demanding diametrically opposed 'freedoms' and 'rights'. I believe that this is not so: what women consistently seek is the freedom to live our bodies as part of our 'selves', the freedom to make sexual and reproductive decisions appropriate to our social, economic, physical and psychological needs. And whether that entails having more or fewer or no children, it is always about women's capacity and right to exercise choice.

The issue of abortion and its bitterly divisive politicisation over the past twenty years is just the most recent chapter in the long history of women's fight for freedom. Abortion has become the late twentieth century arena for the playing out of a power struggle between the sexes - a struggle which has always been waged on women's bodies, whether through reproductive control, through violence and violation or through other forms of bodily appropriation.

The disconnection of procreation from sexual activity through the development of relatively safe and reliable contraception is one of the most significant discoveries of the twentiethth century. Women now hold, at least in principle, the means to control their fertility and - again in principle - are free to choose if and when they will reproduce.

Recently, Susan Faludi recorded the extent of male distress, anxiety and fear at the shift in the balance of sexual power:

Having secured first the mass availability of contraceptive devices and then the option of medically sound abortions, women were at last at liberty to have sex, like men, on their own terms ... Men who found these changes distressing couldn't halt the pace of women's bedroom liberation directly, but banning abortion might be one way to apply the brakes. If they couldn't stop the growing numbers of women from climbing into the sexual driver's seat, they could at least make the women's drive more dangerous - by jamming the reproductive controls. (1991)

As male control of women weakens, their efforts to tighten the reproductive screws become more desperate and cruel. In Ireland, the screws are being turned so tight that women are deprived of the basic freedoms that all men, irrespective of class, take for granted in a democracy: the rights to freedom of assembly, freedom of expression and freedom of movement.

I am tired of being admonished to be 'reasonable', to avoid extremism, not to 'polarise' the debate. These admonitions are pointless because abortion inevitably brings into confrontation opposing views of the place of women as social subjects, where compromise is not a practical option. It is impossible to enter into a reasonable dialogue with the forces of unreason, as anyone who has ever been confronted by a fanatical anti-abortionist barrage knows to her cost. Meanings are twisted and deformed beyond reason, words are used as weapons to damage and discredit the intentions of the speaker. But we must not, as women and as feminists, allow ourselves to be neutralised into acquiescence or intimidated into silence.

Women in Ireland must say 'no' to any Protocol, law or referendum which would limit our rights as citizens, as women, as social and moral agents. We must say 'no' to any and all onslaughts on our integrity as women and as citizens of Ireland and of Europe. Abortion is a need. Only women, whose bodies and minds and hearts bear its full impact, can determine what that need means and how it should be met.

Ailbhe Smyth
June 1992

This is the text of a speech made to the women-only meeting: 'Women's Voices - Women's Choices' organised by Cork Repeal the Eighth Amendment Campaign, 4 June 1992.

Home and Away
The Unequal Vista for Irish Women

The Need for Accommodation
Some right of abortion is the norm in almost all western liberal democracies. This is not a symptom of their basic evil and corruption. It is an inevitable outcome of their attempts to come to terms with the inclusion of women as equals in a free society. It seems that some supporters of the Eighth Amendment to our Constitution are prepared, for the sake of international relations, to make a practical accommodation that allows any woman (who can afford it), for any reason, to seek an abortion abroad. So they claim to believe that a certain teaching on abortion should be binding on all but are prepared to act (or refrain from acting) as if they did not. That will seem like moral hypocrisy to many on both sides of the debate.

But if there is some credible way of reconciling the belief on abortion enshrined at Art 40.3.3 with a practical accommodation that permits abortion abroad, why cannot there be a practical accommodation permitting abortion here, at least for a range of cases encompassing rape, incest, and substantial risks to the normal capabilities for life and action of the woman. Such an accommodation is necessary and desirable on grounds of our equal citizenship under a democratic republican form of government.

It is necessary because a case for some right of abortion follows from the inclusion of women as equal members of our (European) political culture. As equal citizens women claim the rights basic to this culture, including the right to life and the right to control one's own body. Both of these basic rights can be enjoyed together by separate individuals. But the fact that foetal life is within the body of a woman means that both basic rights cannot be universalised to women as well as to foetuses. The legalisation of abortion throughout Europe is a response to the equal citizenship claims of women. And a great deal of the basic political values of European culture are already present in our own Constitution, in our claim to self-rule (Art 6) to democratic equality as human persons before the law (Art 40), and the rest of the fundamental rights that help assure the 'dignity and freedom of the individual' (Preamble). This is why opponents of abortion could not trust the Constitution as it stood before the amendment.

But the Constitution is now deeply flawed. It tries to constrain the actions of the state to respect individual rights and freedoms which is the standard modern way of expressing the principle of individual liberty. At the same time it tries to limit that principle in its application to pregnant women by proscribing harm to the foetus. The trouble is that pregnancy is sometimes a serious harm to women and they may reasonably reject the view that they have no part to play in assessing the impact of unwanted pregnancy on their capabilities for normal human functioning. Insofar as their sovereignty over themselves is curtailed a justification has to be provided in terms that they could not reasonably reject. Appealing to the interests of the foetus is a *prima facie* ground but pregnant women can often appeal to the very same set of interests in defence of a claim to abortion, as cases where the life of the mother is at stake testify. Given the equality of mother and foetus in the matter of rights to life, there is a stand-off between foetal interests and those of the mother, which leaves the state in no position to establish the balance of interests. The person best placed to make that judgement is the mother, or the mother in conjunction with her appropriate guardians in the case of a pregnant child. And this is the good constitutional sense in the Supreme Court judgement permitting abortion in the X case.

But the state is wedded not merely to the lives of mothers but to their equal treatment as citizens. It cannot make out a case for limiting the rights of women to control their own bodies without denying their equal citizenship with men in the matter of individual liberty. And it cannot appeal to a right to life of the foetus which trumps the right to reproductive control of the mother without taking sides on a moral issue which is bitterly contested. We do

150

not have a 'shared understanding' on the status of the foetus. If the state does outlaw abortion (rather than regulating its proper practice) it sets itself up as a moral arbiter in a matter on which it is no more competent to judge than in the case of the 'true' religion. The foundations of the modern state in respect of individual liberty and equality simply do not support the attempt to impose contested religious, philosophical or moral views.

A practical accommodation on abortion in Ireland is desirable because as long as abortion is an issue about the control of women's lives there is no moral space in the emotional economy of many pregnant women for arguments from opponents of abortion. Neither side on the issue could doubt that something of great moral significance is thereby lost.

Practical accommodation is not a problem for those who think that abortion is wrong but acknowledge that there is reasonable disagreement on the matter. They think now that women should be allowed to travel abroad. But this attitude is not consistent with requiring the Constitution to reflect a belief about which there is reasonable disagreement.

Article 40.3.3
The equal rights to life of foetus and woman asserted at Art 40.3.3 are not compossible if women are to be treated as equal citizens. The foetus is given more than normal exemptions and immunities while the right to life of the woman, as currently interpreted, preserves only the material substructure of her humanity, her physical life. She has no claim therefore to consideration of her needs as a human person as that is given by the image of humanity which is the basis of democratic citizenship in a republic.

Equal membership of a self-governing republic is based on the idea that individuals have natural moral competence to determine how best to live out their separate and collective lives. If as individuals we lacked that competence we would have to settle for rule by the wise and the holy. But it is the whole basis of the modern answer to the question: who rules us? People are rightful authors of their own lives and the form of their common life, because everyone has the human capacity to form a meaningful life for themselves.

This image of what it is to be human focuses on activities of a higher order than physical life. These are the activities by which humans distinguish the human aspect of their lives from the animal. They are displayed in the effort to form meaningful lives for ourselves rather than live by the lives set out for us by others, and in the effort to reach and abide by political agreements that tolerate our different answers to the question of the good life.

Respect for individual capacity to identify the good and to give justice to others takes the form of talk of rights in the western political tradition. Schemes of rights, liberties, and opportunities are designed as means to a common life which respects individual self-authorship as a highly valuable and distinctive human activity. There can be no valid interpretation of rights in this tradition that neglects the account of what it is to be human they are framed to secure. For that is the basis of our status as a democracy with pretensions to respect individual dignity and freedom.

Now Art 40.3.3 is either (a) inconsistent with the equal citizenship of women under the Constitution generally in which case it should be deleted, or (b) consistent with women having lesser citizenship, in which case it should be deleted, or (c) consistent with equal citizenship in which case it is hollow, for equal citizenship translates into a case for at least a limited right of abortion to secure women's capacity to participate in the human life of the community.

Let us suppose that equal citizenship specified by a set of fundamental rights is offered to all actual and presumptive members of our political community, as human persons. The question is whether we can make good on our invitation to the unborn to membership in cases where doing so would gravely risk the human character of the woman's life as humanity is understood and defended in our public charter. Before we can vest an unconditional or any right to life in the unborn in recognition of its value we have to know whether that is possible within the language system of rights.

Consider then a sketch of one familiar type of argument for the right to life of the unborn. (i) A human embryo is human life; (ii) all human life has a claim (a right) against others not to kill; (iii) it follows that the human embryo has a claim against its host that she not kill it. Both (ii) and (iii) need defence.

We might say that (ii) follows from taking the embryo to be a person. But the problem is that it looks to most people as if all that can mean is that the embryo will be a person. And they go on to ask: how can what will be a person have the same rights as a person?

But even if (ii) can be established to the satisfaction of some, by religious argument, say, (iii) does not follow. To get from the premise that the embryo has a right to life against the mother to a conclusion about what she may not do, additional argument is necessary, perhaps to the effect that the claim of the foetus is absolute, or nearly so, that nothing less than a grave threat to the mother's life could defeat its claim. I by-pass the question of whether there is a broadly credible defence of an absolute right to life of the unborn. For, even if there is it cannot be fitted into a system of compossible rights designed to sustain democratic republican values.

A system of compossible rights is one where the enjoyment of the system by any individual cannot conflict with its enjoyment by another. For example, if all rights in a system are rights to be let alone, then one person's enjoyment of rights cannot conflict with another's. A liberal democratic republic is based on the value of self-government in individual and social life. Its system of compossible rights can never make any right absolute for that would give one bearer unconditional power over another, reproducing the kind of power relation a republic rejects.

Now if the right to life of the unborn recognised at Art 40.3.3 in our Constitution is absolute or nearly absolute (or whatever it has to be to be consistent with vesting a similar right in the mother) we have to think of the pregnant woman as less than fully human to get a compossible set of rights. In other words a woman who becomes pregnant has to forfeit her claims as an equal citizen to determine for herself the sacrifices she will make for the sake of another. Her claims to share in the human character of the life of the community - the life of self-authorship it offers to all citizens as human persons - have to be reduced to mere physical well-being for it to be possible for the community to offer the unagreed use of her body to the foetus as its route to birth.

Underlying this move is an arbitrary preference for the foetus over the mother, facilitated no doubt by social attitudes which depreciate women's interests in shaping their lives. When what is at stake is whether we may join a new member to the community at the expense of the mother's enjoyment of the health and well-being she needs for a free life, we need argument rather than assertion to justify preference for the foetus.

And note that there is an arbitrary preference for the life of the foetus over that of the mother, because the assertion of equal rights for both is a sham, as interpreted by the Costello judgement *(High Court judgement in the case of 'X', February, 1992)*. The right to life of the mother is to physical survival while the right of the foetus is to all the nurture it needs to develop into a fully participating member of the community. If an unwanted pregnancy could be removed from the mother and kept alive by technology but at the grave risk to its future mental health and stability we would scarcely think that its right to life had been vindicated. So what is pitted against the mother's right to life is the unborn's opportunity not merely for life but for meaningful life. Why should this be vindicated for the unborn ahead of the mother's claims when the two conflict? Perhaps it is right to prefer the human life of the unborn. But we need a defence of this.

The inequality of rights is obscured because what looks like a debate about the fate of the unborn, conducted with the mother as a mere bystander, is in fact a debate about the meanings of women's lives. The conflict is about two different social worlds and the aspirations for women that those worlds support. Vesting the unborn with an absolute right to life can be thought consistent with the mother's equal right to life only if our image of woman confines her to a natural and social role of reproduction and nurture. If she has a duty to permit the unagreed use of her body by the unborn no matter what, its claim against her has to look like it doesn't treat her as a mere means but as an end also.

The trick is performed by supposing that her natural human identity and proper social role is reproduction. Thus she is not used as a means toward an end outside herself. Reproduction is her dominant end. Her right to life is to what she needs to fulfil her given natural and social role. This latent understanding of woman is what lies behind the judgement that all that is relevant to the defence of a woman's right to life when assessing the strength of the right of the unborn is its impact on her physical life. But if woman is not defined in this way, if she has valid aims and interests other than reproduction, then there is no automatic duty to sustain the life of the foetus when circumstances put at grave risk her ability to pursue these. Since the background theory of liberal democratic rights gives individuals the final say over their bodies and lives, it treats this situation as the tragic conflict it is, to be dealt with by allowing the woman herself to decide, in the circumstances of her life, what is best overall.

There is a line of argument which rejects this way of formulating the issue because it disputes the presupposition that women (or men) may determine the meanings of their lives. Instead it holds that the meaning of life is laid down in advance for us to discover and attune ourselves to. Consistently with this view it denies the good of modern democracy and would work to overthrow it in favour of a return to the Ancient Greek *polis*, or to the medieval world. Meanwhile, women's insecure place in the social structures of modern democracies makes the abortion issue a suitable occasion for rolling back the modern conception of individual autonomy. So, more is at issue here than the single issue of abortion. The regime of democracy itself is at stake.

An approach which involves the rolling back of democracy does not recommend itself to those who, however uncertain they are about various aspects of democracy, do not doubt that it is better than the known alternatives. Democracies handle disputes about religious, moral, and philosophical ideals by accepting the good faith of the disputants, providing space for peaceful persuasion, and declining to enforce any view of human happiness or the ends of life.

I have not been arguing the moral rights and wrongs of abortion. It is a highly contested moral issue and not therefore one which can be handled within a Constitution to which all citizens can reasonably consent. I have been pointing out sources of some of the conflicts that give rise to reasonable complaint about legislation banning abortion. Considering the impact of such legislation on the status of women, its conflict with the image of human life on which our model of the democratic citizen is based, and the fact that many citizens are unpersuaded by the anti-abortion argument, the state cannot be asked to make criminal in all circumstances a practice which thousands of Irish women resort to anyway. If the state is not prepared to meet the needs of those members, they rightly cry: whose state is it anyway?

Attracta Ingram
1992

An earlier version of this essay appeared in The Irish Times, 26 and 27 February, 1992.

As Far as Practicable

'I am being asked to decide about a non-existent unborn child and a non-existent pregnant woman,' said Justice Hamilton. Nell McCafferty sat through the four days of argument, supposition, hypothesis, high drama and farce as SPUC's attempt to prevent the Well Woman Centre and Open Line Counselling advising women on how to procure abortions in Britain came before the High Court (1986).

Liam Hamilton, president of the High Court, went to Mass on Monday morning, with all the other luminaries of the Irish legal system. The mass marked the opening of the courts for business, after the summer holidays. Next day, Tuesday, 7 October, a hand-written sheet, affixed like a fly-poster to the door of Court Number One, in the Four Courts, proclaimed Mr Hamilton's business. The Society for the Protection of the Unborn Child (SPUC) versus the clinics would be heard before him, starting at two in the afternoon. Roll up, roll up.

They did, and the court was packed and the proceedings began at two precisely. The high drama was punctuated almost at once by an element of farce. As a lawyer for the Well Woman Clinic mentioned the Treaty of Rome, invoked the European Court of Human Rights, and reached for a weighty book, an elderly barrister stepped out of the crowd and asked the Justice to consider another case entirely. He had been queuing since before two, said the barrister. Had Dickie Rock interrupted the opening scene of *Hamlet*, on the first night in the Abbey, to sing *Candy Store*, the effect could not have been more deflating. Justice Hamilton did not conceal his annoyance. 'You need only look around you to see what I'm facing,' he voiced his mood.

The barrister persisted, and the audience availed of the disruption to look around at each other. The women of the clinics sat in one row and the women of SPUC sat in

157

another. The benches were filled with supporters of both sides, some wearing flowers in their lapels, others wearing the notorious gold-plated reproductions of foetal feet. These symbols apart, the physical difference between the two sides was cruelly obvious. The clinic women and their supporters were vibrantly youthful, clearly of child-bearing age. The SPUC women and their colleagues were markedly older, their child-bearing days long gone. The comparison invited nightmarish stereotyping, and muttered comments over the next four days of the case, as people streamed out for coffee or lunch, confirmed that the bitterly wounding years of the 1981-83 abortion campaigns had left an unwomanly legacy.

'They couldn't provide enough tissue between them to make one uterus,' an onlooker attacked the SPUC women. 'The clinics encourage whoredom in Kimmage,' said an acid observer of Open Line Director Ruth Riddick's red hair, red lipstick and fingernails, red handbag and red shoes. Woman's compassion for woman, betrayed when a member of SPUC walked into the clinics and falsely pleaded an unwanted pregnancy, had reached the end of its tether in the courtroom. There was no noticeable wave of sympathy for Bernadette Bonar, the anti-abortion and anti-divorce leader of Responsible Society. Her husband died just days before the case began. Her face was pale with sadness. She slept while the lawyers spoke.

The real legacy of those years when the nation tore itself asunder was made abundantly clear in the High Court as Justice Hamilton and his assembled men of law briskly agreed that if one thing was certain, it was this: nobody knows what the Eighth Amendment to the Constitution means. The words that racked the people now had the lawyers on the rack, comfortable though it was at one thousand pounds per man per day, and they freely exchanged expressions of sympathy with each other and with the Justice before whom they elegantly tortured their brains as they pondered those words: *The state acknowledges the right to life of the unborn, and, with due regard to the equal right to life of the mother, guarantees in its laws to respect, and as far as practicable by its laws to defend and vindicate that right.*

The state, in the form of Dáil politicians, had huffed and puffed about that guarantee, all sound and fury signifying nothing, the lawyers assured each other. The politicians had not passed one single law since then that would guarantee the right to life of either mother or child. All legal men had to guide them was the 1861 Offences Against the Person Act, outlawing abortion. As regards new laws 'the short answer is no ...,' said Hugh O'Flaherty for SPUC. From a legal point of view, the Eighth Amendment had not 'advanced the situation any more than already existed,' added Anthony Kennedy, also for SPUC. However, he pointed out, if the politicians had not helped the unborn, they had at least been prevented, through the amendment, from harming them. It was agreed that the clinics had not broken the law of 1861. They were not performing abortions. They were doing no wrong in that respect, but the people, said SPUC, had a right to defend the unborn against what the clinics actually were doing. The Director of Public Prosecutions could find no reason or evidence on which to charge them with criminal activity but 'where there is a right, there is a remedy,' said Kennedy, and the remedy sought by SPUC was a court order forbidding the clinics to give information about abortion.

SPUC held that by giving out such information the clinics failed to vindicate the right to life of the unborn; and that by distributing pamphlets which actively encouraged women to come there for pregnancy counselling, the clinics were actively procuring and assisting pregnant women in Ireland to travel abroad for abortion, or receive advice on abortion. SPUC also contended that by their activities, the clinics were conspiring to corrupt public morals. Tony Kennedy cited examples of corruption that were morally repugnant to the Irish people - attempts to entice young girls under fifteen to leave the father's house and engage in fornication; attempts to introduce women into prostitution; and now this. Mr Hugh O'Flaherty for SPUC said the option of having an abortion carried out should not be mentioned, debated or advised on.

The emphasis on the right to life of the unborn brought several quiet interruptions from Justice Hamilton. 'Does the question of the legal right to life of the mother come in?' he asked. This question worried and nagged him, and he threw it first to one side, then the other. 'Of course,' said SPUC, 'the mother has the right to life as well. But leaving that aside ...' The Justice would not let any of them leave it aside. He did not see, he said, how he could consider one aspect of the amendment without taking the other aspect into consideration. If both the mother and the unborn child had rights, and a decision had to be made about which of them had the superior right, 'Who is to make that decision?' he wanted to know. 'It is extremely difficult,' confessed SPUC. 'We don't know who ...' However, said Hugh O'Flaherty, abortion could not under any circumstance be performed in the Republic, and the question, he inferred, was academic.

The Justice did not think it was academic at all. 'The Constitutional rights of the unborn are being interfered with within this jurisdiction. In many cases, pregnancies are being terminated to protect the health of the mother.' Does it not happen frequently, he badgered SPUC? It wasn't spoken about, 'because everybody's turned a blind eye to it'.

The court did not speak about it in detail, either. The lawyers turned their eyes to other aspects of the case. Two days later, the Justice returned to the problem. 'What are the circumstances in which a pregnancy can be terminated?' he asked Tony Kennedy. 'That is the seemingly insoluble dilemma of the Eighth Amendment,' responded Mr Kennedy.

By the fourth and final day, SPUC had come up with an answer of sorts. No evidence had been presented to the court that pregnancies were terminated in Ireland, said O'Flaherty. The Justice was assuming medical knowledge. 'I am assuming medical practice,' said the Justice. 'There's certainly no evidence, but I don't live in an ivory tower'. 'If we are going to get into the larger area of cultural practice,' said Mr O'Flaherty, then SPUC reserved the right to call medical evidence. At the back of the court sat a doctor, newly arrived, who campaigned for SPUC during the anti-amendment years.

Neither the Justice nor Mr O'Flaherty ventured into the larger area. In the corridors outside, the public speculated about the cultural practices and ivory towers and blind eyes alluded to. It was assumed that Justice Hamilton had in mind the termination of ectopic pregnancies, which occur regularly in the Republic. An ectopic pregnancy means that the fertilised egg is stuck in the fallopian tube, and cannot fall down into the womb. If allowed to grow in the tube the egg would become a foetus, then an unborn child which would burst itself, the tube and the woman asunder. In Catholic hospitals here, doctors may remove the tube containing the fertilised egg. Culturally and theologically speaking, the Church argues that this operation does not constitute an abortion. The primary intent and effect is the removal of a diseased organ, the fallopian tube. The secondary and unintentional effect is the termination of the pregnancy.

In England, this is called an abortion.

A woman with an ectopic pregnancy is entitled to information about her condition of course, and advice on how to deal with it within the Republic. The Health Act specifically states that information about abortion is legally available and may be given, provided a licence to give such information is sought from the Minister. Irish hospitals have not taken up the invitation to apply for such a licence. The formal implications of having one are that certain cultural procedures might be deemed to be abortifacient.

Justice Hamilton approached the matter in another way. He asked if there could be lawful discussion on the question of whether a pregnancy could be terminated, having regard to the Eighth Amendment.

'I think there can,' admitted Tony Kennedy for SPUC. 'I think so, too,' said the Justice. However, he pointed out, Mr Kennedy's SPUC colleague, Hugh O'Flaherty had said no. Mr Kennedy argued that Mr O'Flaherty meant there could be no discussion where there was intent to have an abortion, regardless of the circumstances.

The clinic lawyers argued that the clinics neither counselled abortion or referred women to England for abortion. The clinics merely told pregnant women of all the options open to them: a pregnant woman could have her child and keep it, or have it fostered, or have it adopted, or have the pregnancy terminated. Such information, said Peter Maguire for Well Woman, did not bring a pregnant woman 'any closer to abortion than when she came to the clinic. Indeed, when she leaves the clinic she may decide not to have an abortion'. The clinics could not refer women to England for abortions, as alleged by SPUC. They could only refer them to English clinics 'for further pregnancy counselling,' and the English clinics might decide, after consultation with one such woman that she was not entitled to have her pregnancy terminated, or she might decide herself not to have an abortion. It followed logically from such procedures that Irish clinics were not operating as abortion referral centres. They were merely imparting information about services available elsewhere in the EEC, and David Butler argued for the Well Woman that under the Treaty of Rome a person had an absolute right to go to another country and avail of the services which are legally obtainable there. He said that such services must be remunerative, and abortion service in England had an element of remuneration - the woman must pay.

Mr Butler's emphasis on remuneration raised many of the ghosts of the anti-amendment years, and the court proceedings then took a strange turn. Far from arguing, as SPUC once did, that family planning activists were part of a multinational concern to make money and profit out of women's condition, James O'Reilly rose in court, on behalf of SPUC, to assert that the clinics were not in the money-making business, and that the right to avail of services elsewhere did not therefore apply. The clinics provided a service confined to Dublin, he said. If they wanted to plead rights under European Community Law, they would have to show that they carried on business in another state, and this they clearly did not do. There was nothing commercial about abortion, he said.

The lawyers embarked on a tour of the commercial services of Europe, reaching for books and citing cases. Pregnant women and unborn children faded into the background as they talked of a German communist who was refused a postgraduate grant, a Duchess whose Church of Scientology activity led to her expulsion from Britain, an Italian who failed to report that he had hired an *au pair*, and a Dutchman who fought for the right to help cyclists go faster in other countries by accompanying them on a motorcycle.

Nearer home, SPUC insisted that under the Constitution a mother who did not have enough to live on could sue the state for extra maintenance. 'The State shall ensure that no mother shall be obliged by economic necessity to engage in labour to the detriment of her duties in the home.' Supposing, Justice Hamilton mused along this utopian path, a woman went out to her job, found that her children were being neglected as a result, found that when she returned to full-time home duties she was flat broke, supposing ...

The nature of the suppositions took on a back-to-the-future aura. In the absence of an actual mother, or an actual unborn child, warned the lawyers for Open Line, the Justice was being asked to make a decision about 'the unknown unborn and an unknown pregnant woman'.

More than that, added the Justice. He was being asked to decide about a 'non-existent unborn child, and a non-existent pregnant woman'.

No mother was speaking for herself in court, said Paul Carney. And the unborn can't speak for itself, said the Justice. The Justice was listening, in effect, to three limited companies, said Mr Carney. A binding court decision would mean that 'a future mother cannot distinguish herself from a previous mother'.

Frank Clarke, on behalf of Open Line, stressed the 'extra-terrestrial' nature of legal abortion in England. If the Justice were to strike down a woman's right to information about abortion, the consequences would be as bleak as they were entirely impracticable. 'If it must be so, it must be so,' he said, and sketched what it would be. A woman could be restrained from travelling to England, if the court were satisfied that she intended to have an abortion there. A woman could be prevented from permanently emigrating, if it could be shown that she contemplated abortion in the course of her emigration to God knows where. If a foreign magazine, available here, published an article that mentioned the option of abortion, the editor, publisher, directors and journalist could be jailed. Referring obliquely to certain cultural practices, he said that 'having regard to the moral climate in Ireland, it might not be possible for a mother to obtain an abortion here, because it is a matter of common sense and public notoriety that many hospitals have views on what can be done'. If there were circumstances in which abortion could be legally carried out, however, and the rights of the mother, mentioned in the Constitution, implied that there were, 'there must be circumstances when she is entitled to information and advice on whether she qualifies.'

What circumstances? What information? 'Even if such advice were to avoid back street abortion or to avoid inducing by dangerous means?' the Justice asked himself and the lawyers.

The advice would be not to have an abortion, said SPUC.

Women were entitled to information, said the clinics.

'Information which leads to what?' the Justice brought himself back to the unborn who could not speak.

'Are you asking me to substitute myself for the legislature?' the Justice asked SPUC.

'Where parliament fears to tread, it is not for the courts to rush in,' cautioned David Butler of Well Woman.

In the absence of a clear guideline, through laws laid down by the politicians, Anthony Kennedy sought to soothe the raw nerves of the judiciary; a Justice had to do what a Justice had to do. 'As invidious as your role is, it is imposed on you by your Constitutional obligations to do the best you can, in as imaginative, inventive and creative a way as you can do.' His oath of office, obliging him to uphold the Constitution and laws, 'does not leave a lot of room for invention, imagination and genius,' the Justice said when he pondered the advice.

Well Woman lawyer David Butler urged him to have regard for the 'Olympian' clarity of judgement handed down in European Community Law. Tony Kennedy exhorted him instead to be 'Delphic'. The court, he said, was on 'the horns of a dilemma' in this case. If the legislature omitted to clarify a matter, the Justice said, it was of course open to the court to remedy the omission. 'Nobody wants to do it,' he said, almost sadly, but he could see that there was a Constitutional obligation on the judiciary. However, he had 'extreme doubt as to whether I am the arbiter of public morals'.

In many respects, SPUC consoled him, the Eighth Amendment to the Constitution was 'unclear'.

'In many respects?' echoed the Justice sardonically. He said he would give his decision at the end of November. Besides the many unclear aspects of the Eighth, there were six major points to consider. He thanked the 'gentlemen', rose and was gone.

The gentlemen wondered what the six points could be. The women went off to await the verdict. A dozen of them could have been pregnant, of course, and none of the gentlemen would have known.

Nell McCafferty
1986

Abortion and Moral Disagreement

No issue in reproductive ethics is riddled with more fundamental moral disagreement than abortion. Labelling views on abortion is one of the methods commonly used to synopsise and dismiss opposing positions. It is short-hand for the message that 'I don't intend to listen because I know your view already'. Using this counterproductive method, we casually label persons who hold different views on abortion in mutually exclusive categories as 'pro-abortion' or 'pro-life' as if these labels can begin to approach the complexity of understanding, motivations and experiences which inform the diverse views on abortion. The labels effect the opposite: they project negative moral judgements and camouflage the genuine difficulties of the moral and political questions of abortion. 'Pro-life' and 'pro-abortion' labels are a mechanism for avoiding the intellectual work required to re-examine one's own views when faced with disagreement from others. The labels are unhelpful in moving toward clarification of what might be done to accommodate genuine moral diversity which is increasingly a reality in the Republic of Ireland. The co-option of the language of 'pro-life' is particularly offensive, insinuating as it does that any position at variance with a strict prohibition on abortion is 'anti-life'. What is not argued but requires explanation is the understanding of 'life' which permits the conclusion that foetal 'life' morally must be given priority of protection over a pregnant woman's decision that, in terms of her own 'life', she cannot sustain this pregnancy. The disagreements do not diminish by using pejorative labels; these labels merely exacerbate emotional reactions and encourage individuals to adopt more extreme positions than they might otherwise choose.

This radical unease with moral diversity and moral disagreement is a major stumbling block in the abortion issue. It persists as a stumbling block because the reality and extent of moral disagreement is very threatening to many who feel the loss of security in the waning of a presumed moral homogeneity. However, when disagreement about abortion is not accepted as a reality that is here to stay and a reality which requires political accommodation, the reactive tendency is to resort to legal coercion to enforce behaviour in line with the dominant moral ethos. This coercion takes the form of depriving women of non-directive pregnancy counselling, of curtailing pregnant women's freedom to travel outside Ireland to avail of abortion in jurisdictions where women's moral judgement is not maligned. Under a coercive state that refuses to respect moral differences on the matter of reproduction, women effectively have to silence their own insights and ambivalences. Women have to pretend to live by a moral viewpoint which believes it is in possession of the truth and imposing this view on others is warranted. If one believes their own moral viewpoint is infallible, it is only a short move to believing this viewpoint should be made compulsory for all to live by. But the logic of this is never scrutinised. It is one thing to be persuaded about the truth of one's own moral vision and moral beliefs. It is quite another decision, and one requiring separate justification, to decide that other people should be made to live according to my views even if they cannot accept the truth of my views.

The fact of moral disagreement on abortion is a commonplace in most parts of the world and no amount of legal coercion to achieve conformity of behaviour will alter this fact. How a state politically responds to this fact of moral disagreement is revealing of the extent to which democracy in that state can justly accommodate and respect minority views on highly controversial issues. If moral disagreement about reproductive issues is inevitable, as I think it is, then we need to look to a more general value which offers us a principle for proceeding toward political accommodation of moral diversity. Such a principle would be that of tolerance in terms of which individuals who believe that abortion is immoral under all circumstances would not be constrained to act contrary to

167

their beliefs. Likewise, individuals who believe that abortion should be the decision of pregnant women to make would not be constrained to hand over this decision-making to impersonal others.

Appeals to the Majority

We frequently hear reference to the 'majority of the Irish people', the 'will of the ordinary people' who voiced their moral beliefs in the Constitutional referendum of 1983. It is claimed that this democratic, expressed will of the majority has been flagrantly ignored in the Supreme Court decisions in the X case. But two almost certainly false assumptions are concealed in this claim. These assumptions are that this majority view on abortion was both unambiguously clear in its meaning even in 1983 and secondly it is presumed that this majority view has remained static and unaltered over ten years. If these assumptions are almost undoubtedly false, then the appeal to a clear 'collective will of the people' or 'majority moral vision' is an unreliable guide to political resolution. A majority viewpoint speaks loudly when it feels confident that it is a numerical majority. However, that same numerical majority, when placed in a situation where it is a minority can no longer coherently defend a majority appeal without at the same time justifying its own denigration in its newfound minority position! In Ireland an alternative minority voice is continuing to speak out and argue the radical injustice of imposing an alleged majority moral vision in the area of reproductive decision-making. This alternative voice is making a case for accepting the inevitability and respectability of diverse minority positions in the moral domain of reproductive decisions whether they concern contraception, sterilisation or abortion.

Inadequacies of the Appeal to Equal Rights

Disagreements about abortion occur mainly in three areas: the recognition of women as the primary agents in decisions about sexuality and reproduction; the valuation of human foetal life and implications of this valuing and finally, the role of 'experts' in regulating abortion decisions of pregnant women. The influences that determine a person's beliefs in any of these three areas are many and complex but include at least religious, cultural, historical, educational and psychological factors. None of these factors is unchanging and all are inter-related. Since the 1983 Constitutional referendum in Ireland these variable factors have altered considerably. Irish women have also changed in the direction of poignantly recognising the extent to which state institutions (health, ecclesial and legal) dramatically curtail their liberty of decision-making. The recent X case has had the effect of radicalising the awareness of many women to re-examine the dominant language and current ideology of 'equal rights' that guides (or misguides) the abortion debate .The three areas of disagreement mentioned above are all discussed in the 'rights' approach. However, my contention is that this rights analysis, as it is currently presented, is mistaken and does not allow for a humane resolution of abortion as a political-moral issue. We can look briefly at three mistakes in the rights analysis of abortion: (a) It draws unwarranted conclusions from the premise that the foetus is a human person; (b) It disregards the specific life context of decision-making in abortion and interprets the abortion decision as a competitive antagonism between abstract 'holders of rights': the foetus and the pregnant woman. (c) Finally, the rights analysis offered in the abortion discussion leads to the displacement and denigration of women as moral decision-makers. Professionals are co-opted to make these moral judgements since they are presumed to offer the credentials of 'medical expertise', 'impartiality'and 'objectivity.'

Valuing Unborn Human Life
Complete opposition to abortion usually relies on the assumption that the foetus is a human being and a person from the moment of fertilisation. Scientific expertise is sometimes called in to justify this assumption and we are told that the newly fertilised ovum possesses the full DNA (genetic materials) to develop into a fully functioning human being. However, scientific data about the DNA structure of the fertilised ovum cannot provide an answer

to the morality of abortion. We need to make value judgements about the significance of the scientific data. The scientist does not do this for us. To illustrate this point, an experiment has been done with over one hundred embryologists in a conference room who were given basic data on the developing human embryo. All were agreed on the embryological facts. When then asked to write down their personal position on the morality of abortion, there were ten different views expressed, showing that the scientific facts alone are not sufficient to achieve agreement on the moral position of abortion. Accurate embryological data on the developing human foetus is certainly important because it explains the material identity of a human foetus. However, scientific facts do not decide the value interpretation we place on the facts of the foetus or how those facts relate to the complex reality of a pregnant woman's life. By appealing to scientific data as if it can resolve the moral issue of abortion for us, we are camouflaging the essential value judgements about the scientific data. Fundamental disagreements exist about what are the correct value judgements. Science, then, cannot decide the true moral status of the human foetus.

If we decide to grant that the foetus is a person from the moment of conception, how does the argument go from here? One contemporary philosopher, Judith Jarvis Thomson, asks us to consider the following:

Every person has a right to life. So the foetus has a right to life. No doubt the mother has a right to decide what shall happen in and to her body; everyone would grant that. But surely a person's right to life is stronger and more stringent than the mother's right to decide what happens in and to her body, and so outweighs it. So the foetus may not be killed; an abortion may not be performed. (Thomson 1986)

I think it is clearer and less ideologically weighted to talk about the 'pregnant woman' rather than the 'mother' since the language of mother assumes a relationship with a child and a host of other controversial notions about 'motherhood'. Because 'mothering' and 'motherhood' are replete with cultural, historical and religious meanings, this language of 'mother' imports values into the discussion of abortion that is question-begging in the extreme. But Thomson's language aside, her proposed argument sounds plausible and indeed familiar from current debate. But she goes on to show that an absolute prohibition on abortion simply does not follow from a belief that the foetus is a human person. An absolute prohibition on abortion does not follow unless the 'rights claim' about the foetus excludes the context of the pregnant woman's life and adds some very powerful collateral beliefs. The case for not allowing abortion choices by women does not make these collateral beliefs explicit. Because they are left unspoken we are intimidated into thinking that we just don't have the ability to understand the complexity of it all. But this is a moral sleight of hand and should be rejected.

Let's consider why persons, who think abortion is always immoral, believe that the circumstances of conception don't make any difference to decisions about abortion. As the recent X case showed, rape of a fourteen-year-old was not considered a morally extenuating circumstance to justify an abortion. Why? In the case of rape, a woman has not consented to intercourse. Another person has abused and misused her and the sometimes psychologically devastating result is pregnancy. Why would we conclude that the girl must be coerced into carrying the pregnancy to term if she preferred an abortion? Some would argue that while the girl is not at all responsible for conceiving, she may be responsible for the human being conceived even if she believes that there will be serious and long-term adverse consequences for her life. But the girl continues to hear the opposition voice: 'We frequently have to suffer the consequences of behaviour which we in no way intended.' This comment simply dismisses the girl's dilemma with a generalised spiritual bromide which really means that she must (by another's moral viewpoint) accept her pregnancy even when it results from abusive violation by another. The victim is again violated by the moral imperialism of a perspective she may not share at all. The girl's integrity has been violated and we are then coercing her viable options. A rights analysis that results in this conclusion is more than flawed. It results in the 'protection of the foetus' but at the cost of denying the authenticity of the girl's decisions to protect her life in the immediate and long term. A flawed rights analysis only allows the conclusion of coercing a pregnancy because it mistakenly thinks of 'the right to life' as abstract entitlements to protection of biological life, regardless of any circumstances about those lives.

Competitive Antagonisms between Women and Unborn? There are important values at stake in the abortion debate but the value of unborn life has dominated the public discussions and, I think, with the effect of further intimidating many people into silence. Those who believe that a political resolution of abortion should put decisions about abortion into the hands of pregnant women may, at the same time, accept that unborn life is humanly valuable and not to be thought of simply as tissue globules. However, the current concentration on an unqualified right to life of innocent unborn life implies a *negative evaluation of women* who believe that abortion decisions should, nevertheless, be their own decision not to evade or avoid responsibility but precisely to be able to take 'responsibility' for *their own* decision, a decision that takes account of *all human factors, emotions, and moral beliefs involved in any abortion decision.*

The abortion debate has reached an impasse because it continues to be presented as if two equal, and in every respect same, 'rights holders' are in a competitive contest for survival. If we continue to think of brute physical survival of mother and unborn, then we will continue to witness the charade of 'double effect' justifications for 'indirect abortions' which happens to coincide with one version of the Roman Catholic Church's position on abortion. The Roman Catholic Church's history on abortion is, in fact, much more subtle, honest and non-dogmatic. But an assumption operates that ordinary people cannot deal with ambiguity in morals and thus dogmatic positions on abortion become the 'official' position of the Roman Catholic Church.

I am convinced for the reasons discussed above that the prevalent rights analysis of abortion is wrong-headed and misleading. It has us stuck with the hopeless task of adjudicating and balancing rights of impersonal 'rights holders' where any woman who decides on an abortion is viewed as selfish and uncaring.

Displacing Women in Favour of Professionals

In place of acknowledging women's moral authority to make decisions about their reproductive lives, the dominant rights focus requires the mediation of professional experts who are strangers to the moral context of the woman's life. In fact, the prevalent rights analysis of abortion radically displaces the human centre of moral agency where the resolution of abortion decisions should occur. The case is never made for a recognition of women as uniquely appropriate decision-makers about reproduction. Rather, the decision-makers become the professional experts who, by default, become the moral élite judging 'medical necessity' and proceed to judge not only medically but morally when and where women are sufficiently under threat to be entitled to have an abortion.

The national debate has reached a stalemate where the dominant anticipation of many people is for a great deal of divisive animosity and a minimum of insight into the complexity of moral decision-making. Efforts to make a break-through to a new place in understanding seem frustrated by a constant return to the negative message to women that they must perceive themselves as morally incompetent and evil if they look for the liberty to control their reproductive lives. Women's voices have been largely silenced by the sustained arrogant judgements that tell women they are 'murderers of the unborn' if they have an abortion. But women are being encouraged to speak and refute the legitimacy of this sustained negative imaging of them. Women's voices need to be heard telling the truth about their experiences with medical personnel and health-care institutions that have refused to treat potentially life-threatening conditions because such treatment would jeopardise an already existing pregnancy. Such negative consequences for women's moral intregrity are a logical result of a distorted rights analysis of abortion. A difficult task is to restore women's confidence in a state which has maligned her moral capacity to make reproductive decisions and routinely handed these decisions over to strangers. I realise that legislation will be necessary to spell out the implications of the Supreme Court decision in the X case. Minimally legal provisions to allow for counselling, information and travel will be necessary. Beyond that, the terms of 'legally permissible abortion' will need to be decided to protect the value of unborn life at its various stages of development and to affirm the woman's place as central decision-maker in reproduction.

I have argued that the moral debate about abortion will continue to be a stalemate exercise in judgemental labelling of various positions unless we take seriously a pivotal issue of political morality: acknowledging moral diversity in Ireland and adjusting our laws and correcting our Constitution to take this into account. While acknowledging there will always be difficult decisions about the specifics of abortion legislation, I continue to hear the following questions: Who presumes the moral authority to second-guess women's choices about reproduction? Who are the moral masters who will openly declare that they have the certainties on the basis of which women will be constrained in making these choices? These questions will not be silenced but a concerted public effort to answer them might just help to break an impasse in the abortion debate.

Dolores Dooley
June 1992

Procreative Choice
A Feminist Theological Comment

The polarisation of the abortion debate worldwide has been graphically demonstrated in our press over the past few months. The trenchant views expressed by individuals from both sides of the debate do not reflect the views of the population at large where there is great confusion concerning the ethics of abortion. This was revealed, for the first time, to many, by the case of the fourteen-year-old rape victim. A significant segment of the population - including many women - who would have formerly considered themselves to be anti-abortion recognised the difficulties involved in evaluating abortion decisions. For many there is now an ambivalence; on the one hand they hold that human life is sacred from the time of conception, and on the other they recognise that circumstances exist where an unwanted pregnancy may be terminated for significant moral reasons. The consensus we were led to believe existed, that abortion in all circumstances is unjustified, has well and truly unravelled as a direct result of many recognising the intricacies of each ethical dilemma.

For centuries theologians have noted the complex nature of moral decision-making. Issues of life and death have been considered with great precision, considering every detail which might affect the morality of choosing a particular option. Decisions relating to reproduction also need to be treated in such a manner. Rather than reducing the debate to the enunciation of the principle of respect for human life, or to a discussion of when one can attribute full personhood to the foetus, the theological contribution ought to remind us of the difficulties of arbitrating between competing values.

As with all areas in which moral conflict arises there are two distinct issues at stake. In the first instance one must appraise the issue oneself, coming to some general conclusions about the ethical desirability or not of a particular action, recognising of course that no action is moral or unmoral in itself, but can only be evaluated in the context of the intention of the agent, the circumstances she/he finds her/himself in and the consequences, both immediate and long term, which will result. The second factor which must be considered is how such personal convictions should be treated in law[1] (or indeed in medical codes). All societies have to deal with the question to what extent, if any, the religious or moral views of public representatives and of significant majorities ought to determine legislation. It is essential, I would suggest, particularly in Ireland, to recognise that although one's moral convictions are extremely important, and must be considered, personal moral convictions cannot be the sole basis upon which a society legislates for or against the provision of particular medical procedures. Due regard must be given to the views of minorities and pluralism must be valued as conducive to serious moral debate and fundamental to the pursuit of truth in a society. Thus the primacy of the individual conscience ought to be a central value in our deliberations on legislation concerning reproductive issues, with due regard for the requirements of peace and justice in society. The questions to be answered then are firstly whether public representatives have a duty to legislate for the provision of services for individuals who in conscience have chosen a particular option, and secondly, whether the criminalisation of abortion is the most appropriate and effective way of ensuring respect for life and for justice in society.

Christian Perspectives

Moral teaching on abortion in the Christian Churches is diverse so it is difficult, particularly in contemporary society, to enunciate a common Christian perspective. As with all Church teaching, discussion of the morality of abortion has had a long and complex history - with debates ranging from discussions of the moment of ensoulment to the equation of both abortion and contraception with homicide.[2] Whatever the variants, one must conclude that on balance the Christian Churches have for the most part condemned abortion, regardless of the question of the ensoulment of the foetus. This factor, however, was often regarded as important in deciding on the individual woman's culpability in the confessional.

Although one may discern, particularly in Roman Catholic theology, a gradual movement away from the focus on abortion as a sexual sin and towards an emphatic statement of respect for human life from the time of conception, one must keep firmly in mind the dominant posture of the Churches in respect of women. It is impossible to disentangle teaching on reproductive issues from the anti-sexual and anti-female ethos which has pervaded Christian theology. Indeed it reached the nadir of its expression on teaching regarding women's sexuality.[3] This is surely the backdrop against which one must evaluate and critique the various positions of the Christian Churches' commitment to justice and equality.

The Declaration on Procured Abortion[4] (1974) issued by the Sacred Congregation for the Doctrine of the Faith is the most exhaustive recent Roman Catholic statement on the issue.[5] It calls for 'respect for human life from the time that the process of generation begins'.[6] As David Smith notes '[A]lthough not formally teaching that there is human life present from the moment of fertilisation, the document, owing to the risk of murder, rules out all abortions regardless of the stage of foetal development.[7] The Roman Catholic Church then clearly acknowledges that there is serious medical opinion which would rule out the attribution of personhood to the foetus until a particular stage in its development. Nevertheless it imposes an exceptionless veto on the possibility of a pregnant woman ever choosing abortion.

The Church of England statement, *Abortion: An Ethical Discussion*[8] recognises, in contrast, that each abortion decision involves arbitrating between the claims of the foetus and those of the mother. There are therefore, according to the Church of England, circumstances in which abortion can be justified. The statement mentions a threat to the mother's life or well-being, which is integrally connected with the life and well-being of her family, as well as cases of rape or incest.

Theologians from each tradition have variants of the above positions. David Smith[9] mentions the work of James Gustafson who enunciates a position which would be closest to a feminist ethical perspective. Gustafson considers social and political issues to be crucial to evaluating the morality of abortion and provides some guidelines which may further the debate. Stated succinctly Gustafson's position is that:

- *Life is to be preserved rather than to be destroyed.*
- *Those who cannot assert their own rights to life are especially to be protected.*
- *There are exceptions to these rules.*

Possible exceptions are:

(a) *'Medical indications' that make therapeutic abortions morally viable.*

(b) *The pregnancy has occurred as a result of sexual crime. (I would grant this as a viable possible exception in every instance ... if the woman herself was convinced that it was right. If the woman sees the exception as valid, she has a right to more than a potentially legal justification for her decision; as a person she has the right to understand why it is an exception in her dreadful plight.)*

(c) *The social and emotional conditions do not appear to be beneficial for the well-being of the mother and the child. (In particular circumstances, this may appear to be justification, but I would not resort to it until possibilities for financial, social and spiritual help have been explored.)*

A Feminist Theological Perspective

Feminist theologians have attempted to approach ethics in a new way. Reflecting the central concerns of feminist theologians in general, feminist ethicists have sought to situate their theorising in the experience and praxis of women and have essentially redefined the starting points of ethical reflection. The primary resources are no longer scripture and tradition but the contemporary praxis of women who are committed to the establishment of justice and right-relation. Thus feminist theologians have effected an epistemological and a methodological shift - what counts as knowledge, who possesses it and how theoretical reflection ought to proceed are the key questions which are answered in a new way.

This shift has a profound effect on how one deals with all moral issues but is most notable in relation to the ethics of abortion. Once one locates the starting point of ethical reflection in the contemporary experience and praxis of women one is forced to recognise the particularity of each situation. Ethical decisions can no longer (if they ever could) be evaluated as abstract acts, without reference to the life situation of the agent. In the case of abortion, a feminist ethic argues that an unwanted pregnancy always involves significant life-shaping consequences for a woman and cannot be evaluated independently of these.

Beverly Harrison[10] has suggested that the most serious flaw in the 'pro-life' debate is their failure to reconstruct the concrete, lived-world context in which the abortion discussion belongs. She cites John Noonan's discussion and his consistent references to the woman who is faced with an unwanted pregnancy as 'the gravida' or 'the carrier'.[11] This she insists serves to obscure the complexity of the ethical dilemma, and indeed it also harkens back to the days (which we are assured have long passed) in which women were primarily empty receptacles, mobile wombs, valuable for our reproductive capacities.

Any consideration of an abortion decision, from a feminist ethical perspective, would include a discussion of the reason why unwanted pregnancy occurred - whether it be because of ignorance, because of the failure to act responsibly when sexually active, because of contraceptive failure or because of violence. In the discussion such issues are given moral weight, are seen to be central to the evaluation of the act as justifiable or not. So too, the economic, social and medical dimensions of the consequences of carrying the pregnancy to term are considered to be integral to the ethical. One can never then consider the morality of any action in isolation, or independently of the woman, in a matter so intimately connected with her well-being. With its starting point in the experience and praxis of contemporary women, and endowing the context with significant moral weight, a feminist ethical perspective would insist on our recognising the complexity of the abortion dilemma, which can never be reduced to the facile and exceptionless application of a formal principle which in truth points us in a general direction but says nothing about concrete action.

A further cornerstone of the feminist ethical framework is that it considers education for moral autonomy and thereby the enhancement of personhood as a primary goal of ethics. 'Moral autonomy is at once a goal that persons ought to achieve, the basis for moral reflection and action, and an aspect of emerging personhood.'[12] It has indeed been a long held and reputable principle of ethics that in order to be moral, one's actions must be acts of autonomous choice - must be free from coercive force and from ignorance. An essential quality of morality then is that one's actions arise from the core of one's being, are freely chosen and reflect one's fundamental option for good. Only actions freely chosen, only decisions made in the face of real options can be considered to be within the realm of morality, with all the responsibilities which this entails.

But women haven't been trusted as moral agents. In this most intimate area of their lives women have neither the burden of making serious moral decisions nor the life-enhancing possibilities of so doing. An essential element of our humanness involves both the freedom to make, and the responsibility of making, significant moral choices in a way which affirms our commitment to justice and love.

Women are not encouraged to take such moral responsibility for their lives. Patriarchal expectations, enforced through socialisation and education processes, encourage women to behave in an immature and childlike fashion. Protection and economic support from husbands ensured that many women were rarely if ever required to act autonomously or to realise their full self-identity. Even the theological categories of sin and redemption are construed taking cognisance of these traditional roles. Valerie Saiving's influential essay 'The Human Situation: A Feminine View'[13] analyses the classic theological elaboration of our understanding of sin as pride, arrogance, will-to-power. Traditionally sin for women has been failure to take responsibility for one's own life, 'dependence on others for one's own self-definition, in short, underdevelopment or negation of the self'. Without acknowledging the importance of the variable of gender in the human situation, theologians continued to consider sin and redemption without any reference to the difference which one's sexual identity makes to the process.

If the understanding of sin reflected the concerns of men, so too did the understanding of love, its opposite. 'Love is completely self-giving, taking no thought for its own interests ... Love makes no value judgements concerning the other's worth; it demands neither merit in the other nor recompense for itself but gives itself freely, fully ... Love is unconditional forgiveness.'[14] Saiving reminds us that definitions of sin and love are mutually dependent concepts. In so far as such definitions reflect male experience they are important. However, given women's situation in patriarchal culture, any theological doctrine which invokes them to be completely self-giving, without arbitrating, to be unconditionally forgiving etc, without recognising that such features reflect precisely the lives of women under patriarchy, such a doctrine must be evaluated as both redundant and indeed dangerous.

Women's traditional failings (essentially the failure to take responsibility for their own decisions and life-situations) together with the call, based in traditional concepts of sin and redemption, that women become more self-effacing, more self-sacrificing, have resulted effectively in the failure to trust women as competent moral agents capable of rational and serious moral debate. The 'right to choose' slogan, although it does hold some difficulties for a Christian feminist ethic, highlights an important element in all our ethical decisions. The gradual movement of women towards moral autonomy, with due regard for the traditional sources and norms of ethical thinking, is the goal of feminist theological ethics. Only when women are allowed and indeed required to make moral decisions about every aspect of their lives, without hiding behind unquestioned assumptions about the natural woman's role, can we believe that the Churches are in good faith when they speak of justice and equality for women.

Although I have been suggesting that a feminist ethical position would locate the power and the responsibilities of moral decision making firmly with the moral agent, I believe that it is too facile to insist that abortion is purely a private matter. Indeed one sees the difficulty with this in the USA where the *Roe v Wade* decision was based on the right to privacy. Subsequently, and as a direct result of the *Roe v Wade* decision, federal funding was cut off for poor women. Many poor women, black women, hispanic women, have been victims of the liberal feminist victory which located abortion rights solely in the private arena.[15]

A feminist theological ethics, which is rooted in the liberation and political theological tradition, would seriously critique this position. A fundamental principle of feminist theology is that the socio-political is central to our decision making. This effectively allows us to claim that economic, social and political conditions which affect the woman with an unwanted pregnancy are central to the morality of the decision. It must also lead us to recognise however that abortion is not purely a private matter, that it does indeed have grave consequences not only for how we value women's lives, but also how we value foetal life.

It is perhaps because all reproductive rights are under such ferocious attack by the far right that feminist theologians have been forced into a position which fails to take account of the varying economic and social positions of women, which do indeed affect the morality of abortion decisions. No two abortion decisions are the same. Many are made in the face of poverty, violence and betrayal. But to maintain both intellectual and moral integrity we must also accept that an abortion may be the result of a woman's devotion to materialistic values, which comes with an uncritical participation in advanced capitalist economies. In addition to arguing for the situation of ethical power with the moral agent, a feminist theological ethic must unambiguously critique the acquisitive society with which some women have thrown in their lot in the guise of equality for women. We recognise what Rosemary

Radford Ruether calls the 'interstructuring of oppression', the fact that all forms of domination and exploitation have common roots, and as such are impelled to denounce the economic and social advancement of the few at the expense of the poor, the uneducated and so on.

Once one's rights are under siege it is difficult to be self-critical. The polarisation of the debate has resulted in our failure to constantly re-evaluate our position in a way which recognises the complexity of this issue and the variables which emerge with each dilemma. In addition to advocating women's rights and responsibilities in relation to our reproductive capacities, the feminist theological voice ought to be one of compassion, reconciliation and integrity in the moral domain.

Partly in response to the debate between Geraldine Ferraro and Archbishop John O'Connor of New York concerning the duty of a legislator in relation to the public funding of abortion,[16] Cardinal Joseph Bernardin of Chicago developed what is now called a consistent life ethic.[17] Essentially Bernardin argues that the ethic of a seamless garment will most effectively allow one to develop a posture in defence of human life. Further he insists that opposition to abortion 'anchors a consistent ethic because the unborn child symbolizes the fundamental challenge innocent life poses for individuals and society.'[18] Now although feminists must continue to highlight the fundamental inconsistencies of many who oppose abortion yet support capital punishment, massive spending on arms, opposition to developmental aid and so on, it is futile to continue only to argue against them. Moral integrity is with those who actively espouse a consistent life ethic and as such it is with proponents of this theory that feminist theologians must dialogue.

I have deliberately avoided debates concerning the personhood of the foetus and the weighing up of the rights of the mother versus those of the foetus. Much has been written by theologians and philosophers alike without any real hope of a resolution. A feminist theological ethics avoids such discussions since in reality no two abortion decisions are alike. Rarely do women resort to abortion unless there are life-shaping consequences at stake. Women do not choose abortion lightly, for trivial reasons. Who if not women recognise the value and the vulnerability of nascent life? The dilemma for feminist theologians is to determine, with reference to the uniqueness of each situation, a framework for moral decision making which will ensure the well-being of human life, born and unborn. Respect for human life from conception (which must of course include genuine and active respect for female life - in all its dimensions) is the guiding principle for a feminist ethic. The question then is how to ensure respect for life, given that conflicts frequently occur.

The principle of respect for human life, far from bringing the debate to its conclusion, is but the beginning for feminist ethics. It raises questions about the intrinsic value of human life, of the conditions necessary for human flourishing and of the social policies which render abortion the only just option for many women. A major flaw in most theological discussions of the issue is that the focus has been on an isolated act, divorced both from the social and material context of the woman and from critique of the conditions which force women to make difficult though none the less responsible choices.

The primacy of the individual conscience is a cornerstone of the Christian tradition. Feminist theological ethics, although in no way bound to this tradition, draws on many of its insights. In the abortion debate one might argue that the difficulty lies not in the acknowledgment that in cases of conflicts of interest someone (government, law courts, hospital boards) must decide, but that women claim the right to make the decision for themselves. Choices concerning reproductive capacities can become instances of moral autonomy, of free and faithful commitment to justice, if women have the aid of serious and sensitive moral debate and in the final instance are encouraged and enabled to accept the responsibilities of being born female.

Linda Hogan
June 1992

Notes

1. See the discussion of the relationship between morality and the law from a Roman Catholic perspective in Patrick Hannon, *Church State Morality and Law*, Dublin: Gill and Macmillan, 1992.

2. See the theological development of the opposition to abortion in Beverly Harrison, *Our Right to Choose: Toward a New Ethic of Abortion*, Boston: Beacon Press, 1983, in particular the chapter entitled 'Notes Toward a Feminist Perspective on the History of Abortion'.

3. For an excellent discussion of this see Uta Ranke-Heinemann's *Eunuchs for the Kingdom of Heaven*, Harmondsworth: Penguin, 1990. In her consideration of the Catholic church and sexuality she reveals with great erudition the misogyny which is perpetuated to this day.

4. Austin Flannery (ed), *Vatican Council II: More Post-Conciliar Documents*, Dublin: Dominican Publications, 1984, pp441-453.

5. Many restatements for the Irish context have been made by the Irish Episcopacy. A selection of these texts appear in *Doctrine and Life*, Vol. 42, May/June 1992, pp326 ff.

6. *Declaration on Procured Abortion*, op. cit. , p445.

7. David Smith, 'What is Christian Teaching on Abortion?', *Doctrine and Life*, Vol. 42, May/June 1992, p307.

8. Statement of the Church of England Board for Social Responsibility, *Abortion: An Ethical Discussion*, London: CIO Publishing, 1965.

9. art. cit., commenting on James Gustafson, 'A Protestant Ethical Approach' in *Morality of Abortion: Legal and Historical Perspectives*, J. Noonan (ed) London: Harvard University Press, 1977, p116.

10. Beverly Harrison, 'Theology and Morality of Procreative Choice' in *Making the Connections: Essays in Feminist Social Ethics*, Boston: Beacon Press 1985 p123.

11. John Noonan, *A Private Choice: Abortion in America in the Seventies*, New York: Free Press, 1979.

12. Carol S. Robb in her introduction to Beverly Harrison's *Making the Connections*, op. cit. pxvi.

13. Valerie Saiving, 'The Human Situation: A Feminine View' in Carol Christ and Judith Plaskow, *Womanspirit Rising A Feminist Reader* in Religion, San Francisco: Harper and Row, 1979.

14. ibid.

15. See the discussion of abortion rights and socialist-feminist politics in Roslind Pollack Petchesky's *Abortion and Woman's Choice*, Great Britain: Verso, 1986.

16. Reporting and analysis of these debated from a theological perspective can be found in *Origins* during and subsequent to the 1984 presidential campaign.

17. A consistent life ethic proposes an ethic which promotes equality and justice in the social and political arena in addition to expressing opposition to abortion in principle.

18. *Origins*, Vol. 14, No. 21, November 8, 1984.

Towards a Feminist Morality of Choice

[My] main object, the desire of exhibiting the misery of oppression, peculiar to women, that arises out of the partial laws and customs of society. (Mary Wollstonecraft, *The Wrongs of Woman*, 1798)

Because the reproductive experience of individuals is such a private affair, we tend to think of such activity as being outside of the realm of law or social policy. However, population questions have, in the last 200 years, become matters of public debate and government action. The decision to permit or prohibit the manufacture, distribution and advertising of contraceptive devices is, for example, a clear demonstration of public law involvement in citizens' private behaviour.

Equally, the existence and nature of abortion laws differ according to prevailing social policy. In China, for example, abortion is an integral part of the state reproductive policy; elsewhere, restricted access to abortion reflects a social commitment to population expansion. In Ireland, the existence of an anti-abortion law, bolstered by a Constitutional guarantee of the right to life of the unborn, is an unambiguous statement of public policy, irrespective of the private practice of silent thousands of our 'criminal' citizens (women).

Such questions of social policy very often also raise the spectre of race survival. Dreadful experiments into human reproduction were carried out on persons of expendable race in Nazi concentration camps, while abortion was denied to Aryan women, who were encouraged to breed a 'pure' race. Some Black male activists in the USA have argued against women's reproductive freedom, seeing contraception and abortion as tools of genocide. Similar fears have been expressed in regard to family planning programmes in the Third World. Meanwhile, wealthy right-wing organisations exhort white, middle-class French women to increase the size of their families; educated, middle-class women in Hong Kong are offered financial advantages to the family if they have children. In Ireland, the 'right to life' movement lobbies for subsidies for nuclear families (usually middle-class) at the expense of the single-parent unit (often working-class, certainly financially and socially disadvantaged).

Behind all of these initiatives lies a single, shared, premise: only certain people have the right to breed. And who decides? Not the individual woman - this is patriarchy, after all - but an assortment of outside agencies: the racist ideology, the right-wing pressure group, the authoritarian state. Behind the premise lies the same fear: if we don't breed enough, the hated others ('the yellow peril') will take us over. The American anti-abortionist, Fr Paul Marx, whose speciality is a pickled-foetus roadshow, neatly summarises this viewpoint thus: 'The white western world is committing suicide through contraception and abortion' (Human Life Centre, Minneapolis, USA).

'[T]he preservation of life seems to be rather a slogan than a genuine goal of the anti-abortion force,' writes Ursula K LeGuin. 'Control over behaviour; power over women. Women in the anti-choice movement want to share in male power over women and do so by denying their own womanhood, their own rights and responsibilities' (1989).

If individual actions take place within society, within ideology, the question of moral agency comes into focus when we encounter fundamental conflicts in the moral arena, as in the problematic area of maternal versus (proposed) foetal rights, where the social imperative is weighted against the woman. The greater the claim of the foetus (an entity which clearly cannot enter moral debate on its own behalf, a not inconsequential factor when personhood has been traditionally linked to the capacity for consciousness and decision), the more important the recognition of women's moral agency, of she who must bear the moral responsibility of her actions. The so-called 'right to life' movement argues unambiguously that, while women may have a pragmatic choice of action in pregnancy, they have no right to moral agency; that is, that the foetus's claim self-evidently overwhelms any proposed moral agency in women. (Mary Daly (1973) adds that, according to this view, aborted foetuses are to be more mourned than adult human beings killed in war.)

In pregnancy, this struggle for control and responsibility is manifest in the issues which women confront, the 'hard' questions raised in non-directive pregnancy counselling:
• what are the viable options in your situation?
• how will you cope with your grief/anger/guilt? - whatever your decision
• how will you reconcile your decision with your conscience/god/religion?
• how would you feel after an abortion?

Social services correspondent Mary Maher writes:

The phrase 'non-directive' has become fairly familiar as a description of that kind of therapeutic help which offers a client neither advice nor judgement, but a sympathetic ear ... [The] conviction is that people can make choices, good choices, for themselves, and have the right to do so, and that the therapist is there only to facilitate that process ... Basic assumptions from which client-centred therapy springs [are] ... that the individual is basically trustworthy, has the capacity and the right to make decisions about life, and the ability to establish a set of values ... Most important, they take responsibility for those choices, a necessary part of the growth process. (*The Irish Times*, 20 November 1986)

For Irish women choosing termination, and given our particular cultural heritage, moral exercise is located in the recognition of a *prima facie* right to life of the unborn which may only be overridden with justification, or good reason, to be provided by the pregnant woman herself.

Apart from surveys undertaken by Open Line Counselling, there has been little study of the abortion experience of Irish women, or of the reasons why Irish women choose abortion as an option in crisis pregnancy. Commenting on her decision to terminate her pregnancy, one Irish woman wrote: 'I would still like to think I can have a good life. I intend to go back and start anew and I don't regret my decision.' A common theme running through women's decision-making process concerning a crisis pregnancy is worry about how the pregnancy, if brought to term, would affect others, principally parents and existing children. Summarising the reasons given for considering abortion, Open Line Counselling reported as follows:

Many younger women feel unprepared for a child, particularly where family and social support is unlikely or insufficient. Many women are also anxious to avoid causing hurt to their parents, especially where a parent has health problems. Older women are worried about the effects of another pregnancy on a grown family, and also about the possibility of a sub-normal child. Instability in the relationship with the putative father, whether casual acquaintance, ex-boyfriend, or where a marriage is under stress, is another common factor.

Separated women with an extra-marital pregnancy are concerned about the irregular status of their relationship with the putative father and also about the threat to their separation agreements if the husband is unsympathetic to the pregnancy. Professional women are increasingly concerned about their future training and employment prospects, particularly in nursing and teaching. Most women decide to seek termination of pregnancy because of a multiplicity of these pressures. (October 1983)

While children born out of wedlock are no longer stigmatised in law as 'illegitimate', post-referendum Ireland has not been notable for its regard for its mothers. A number of tragic cases, from the death in childbirth of a fifteen-year-old girl to the sacking of a teacher for giving birth to the child of a separated man, have come to light since the Human Life amendment of 1983. The lessons of these cases, and the social attitudes they reveal, are not lost on other women with unplanned pregnancies.

Although not all of these considerations will be foremost in a woman's mind when she is exploring her options in a crisis pregnancy, they help form the context in which her decisions must be made. Furthermore, in a patriarchal society, there is the problem of the role of men in women's lives which is at best ambiguous, at worst, fatal. In the social arena and mirroring women's domestic responsibilities, the so-called 'caring' professions are, at the helping level, almost exclusively staffed by women. Primary care is given by women; status and authority is male.

On a more sinister level, the European witchcraze of

1450-1750, described by Matilda Joslyn Gage in 1893 as 'the age of supreme despair for women', saw the slaughter by men of a minimum of 200,000 women. In the 1970s a new genre of pornography, depicting the real-life murder of women by men, 'snuff movies', brought the witchcraze to the domestic video screen. Men rape, murder, abandon, dominate, disenfranchise women.

Successful women, riding on the achievements of feminism, boast that they are 'just one of the boys', that women 'make dreadful bosses', that as a woman you have to be twice as good but so what? When was the last time a patently high achieving male boasted that he was 'just one of the girls'? For all our delirious need to believe that men like us, respect us, treasure us, the evidence suggests to the contrary. 'He's just a woman,' is a term of abuse, not of respect. And where there is no liking, no respect, there is instead fear and loathing; there is unlikely to be any acknowledgement of rights, of agency, certainly no espousal, no guarantee.

These considerations become acute when women are faced with a crisis pregnancy. By definition, women become pregnant only through congress with men (messenger doves notwithstanding). Men are present in pregnancy, even though one of the common factors in crisis pregnancy is the absence of a man. At its crudest level, this absence is manifest in the man who denies his contribution to the pregnancy: 'It's not mine.' On a manipulative level, it's the man who decides what is to be done: 'the obvious thing is for you to have an abortion, (lover/husband); 'I've decided she's to have an abortion' (father).

At its most compassionate, it's the man who withdraws completely from the situation: 'It's her decision.' The problem with this last is that it may, although by no means always, mask a retreat from involvement, it may be a refusal to commit. It is often a position taken by men who are not married to the pregnant woman; husbands tend to have more emphatic opinions (as befits their role as patriarchs) and expect their opinion to prevail, even where these opinions are in conflict with their wives' convictions.

How a man reacts to a crisis pregnancy will have a direct effect on the woman's experience of the pregnancy as the circumstances from which the pregnancy arises are crucial to the woman's moral classification of it; women are most reluctant to carry to term the product of a rape and equally reluctant to abort the product of a loving relationship. Even in their absence, men are present. Even in this most elemental of female spheres, men are still an inescapable consideration.

For this reason, and by way of the generosity of women in their moral inclusion of men, women are acutely vulnerable to exploitation and manipulation. Consider this exhortation from Fr Bernard Haring concerning women pregnant from rape:

We must, however, try to motivate her to consider the child with love because of its subjective innocence, and to bear it in suffering through to birth, whereupon she may consider her enforced maternal obligation fulfilled, after which she would try to resume her life with the sanctity that she will undoubtedly have achieved through the great sacrifice and suffering.

This is most sophisticated cruelty. Compare it with this account from the life of the Irish saint, Brigid:

A certain woman who had taken the vow of chastity fell, through youthful desire of pleasure, and her womb swelled with child. Brigid, exercising the most strength of her ineffable faith, blessed her, caused the foetus to disappear, without coming to birth, and without pain. She faithfully returned the woman to health and to penance. (Liam de Paor)

Fathers of foetuses are now legally permitted (to at least attempt) to stop women from having abortions, or to insist on caesarian deliveries. Men are in a position to threaten women with withdrawal of material and emotional support if the woman does not abort a pregnancy which is unwanted by the man. These are positions of great power: personal, social, political. In the patriarchy, these positions are continually open to unchecked abuse.

Contemporary feminism, as we have seen, has developed a unique system of 'self-help' networks and whereas 'self-help' is a process common to oppressed peoples, for feminism, the personal is political and 'self-help' is no less than the conscious response to women's perceived and stated needs; that is, a political intervention into patriarchal society on behalf of women, not only as individuals, but as a class. This response is possible only when based on listening - to ourselves and to other women. For feminism, this intervention is more than political, it is a moral commitment. Respect for women is a central dimension of this commitment; that is, a respect which acknowledges and celebrates moral agency in women.

The opposition to non-directive pregnancy counselling and the threats to other woman-centred services and activities are ideological and rooted in patriarchal philosophy. Evidence suggests they will become even more violent.

Ireland is unusual, although the present legal climate is certainly volatile, in that Irish women have not, in recent times, been jailed for seeking abortion or for helping women to procure abortions (potentially criminal activities under the law). Not that we congratulate ourselves on this record. Women all over the world have been brave enough to risk jail and worse on behalf of their sisters. And, where feminists in the 1970s provided humorous media fodder, proponents of choice in the 1980s are unemployable. Where students in the 1960s were 'revolting', contemporary student publications are the subject of protracted litigation.

The proposition that women have the right to choose does not enjoy favour as Ireland prepares for the federal Europe of the 1990s (where, to the embarrassment of the state, a Court of Human Rights application on these issues will have to be answered, together with a European Court of Justice reference). Equally, a campaign for abortion rights would certainly encounter opposition even from those women who currently seek (lawful) abortion services in Britain. Ten years ago, feminists had the opportunity to campaign - and a gallant bunch did - for the decriminalisation of abortion. Today, a referendum to remove Article 40.3.3 would have to be successful before the issue could be meaningfully raised.

If, as veteran Irish campaigner Mary Gordon contends:

'A measure of the strength of the feminist movement in any country is the strength and confidence of its abortion rights lobby,' a challenge has been issued to the Irish Women's Movement. Now that we have a clearer idea, albeit with the wisdom of hindsight, where the ideological lines are drawn, it is a challenge which we will confront with the greatest urgency.

Ruth Riddick
1990

Contributors

Ursula Barry is a feminist writer, researcher and activist. She is a lecturer in economics at the Dublin Institute of Technology and is the author of *Lifting the Lid*, Attic Press, 1986. She has published many papers and articles on the position of women in Ireland and on the Irish economy and is the Irish representative on the European Community 'Women and Employment' Network.

Pauline Conroy Jackson is a graduate of University College Dublin and the London School of Economics. She lectures in Women and Social Policy at UCD and works for the Central Unit of the European Commission's Third European Anti-Poverty Programme.

Dolores Dooley is a lecturer in Philosophy, Women's Studies and Medical Ethics at University College, Cork. Born and raised in Chicago, Dolores moved to Ireland in 1974.

Linda Hogan is a graduate of Trinity College, Dublin and has recently completed her doctorate in Feminist Theology. She lectures in medical ethics and in feminist theology at various institutions in Dublin. She is on the Editorial Committee of *Womanspirit*, for which she writes articles and reviews.

Attracta Ingram lectures in political philosophy in the Department of Politics at University College Dublin. Her publications include 'The Perils of Love: Why Women Need Rights' in *Philosophical Inquiry* 1988/90. Her book, *A Political Theory of Rights*, is forthcoming.

IWASG was set up in 1981. It is a collective of women from different parts of Ireland, who live in London. We provide information, accommodation and support for Irish women who come to London for abortions. We have links with clinics here and organisations which are active around reproductive rights in England and Ireland.

Nell McCafferty was born in Derry. She now lives in Dublin and works as a freelance journalist. Her books include: *The Best of Nell*, Attic Press, 1983; *A Woman to Blame: The Kerry Babies Case*, Attic Press, 1985; *Goodnight Sisters*, Attic Press, 1987 and *Peggy Deery*, Attic Press, 1988.

Jo Murphy-Lawless is a member of the Irish-based Nexus Research Cooperative. She is also a member of the Centre for Women's Studies, Trinity college, Dublin, where she teaches on the M Phil Programme. She has written extensively on medical discourse and the female body.

Anne O'Connor holds BA, MA and PhD degrees in Irish folklore from University College Dublin. Her doctoral thesis, *Child Murderess and Dead Child Traditions*, was published in the Folklore Fellows Communications series by the Finnish Academy of Science and Letters in Helsinki, 1991. She has concentrated her research in international folk tradition on folk religion and on the folklore of sexuality, childbirth and child murder.

Madeleine Reid specialised as a solicitor in family law and areas of particular interest to women. She was involved in a series of test cases on enforcement of EC sex equality law in Ireland, and her Master's thesis for the European University Institute, Florence, focused on the effect of EC law on traditional Constitutional concepts in Ireland. It was published by the Irish Centre for European Law in 1990 as *The Impact of Community Law on the Irish Constitution*. She lectures in Constitutional and European Community Law in Dublin.

Ruth Riddick has worked with the Irish Family Planning Association, the Well Woman Centre and The Irish Pregnancy Counselling Centre. In 1983 she set up Open Line Counselling which she administered until its closure in 1987, following a High Court injunction currently under consideration by the European Court of Human Rights. She also works as a freelance journalist.

Ailbhe Smyth is Director of the Women's Education, Research and Resource Centre (WERRC) at University College Dublin and has published widely on Irish feminism.

Anne Speed is a full-time official with the trade union SIPTU. She has been active in left-wing republican and feminist politics since the early 1970s and was twice a candidate in local and EC elections. She is the author of many articles published in various radical journals.

Bibliography

Arms, S. (1975). *Immaculate Deception*. Boston: Houghton Mifflin.

Arms, S. (1977). Why women should be in control of childbirth. In D. Stewart & L. Stewart (Eds), *21st Century Obstetrics Now*. Marble Hill: NAPSAC.

Arney, W R. (1983). *Power and the Profession of Obstetrics*. Chicago: University of Chicago Press.

Barker-Benfield, G J. (1976). *The Horrors of the Half-Known Life*. New York: Harper and Row.

Barry, U. (1984) 'Ideology in Crisis: The Anti-Abortion Amendment'. Paper to the Annual Conference of the Sociological Association of Ireland, Co Louth.

Barry, U. 'Abortion in the Republic of Ireland'. *Feminist Review* No. 29.

Beale, J. (1986). *Women in Ireland. Voices of Change*. Dublin: Gill and Macmillan.

Beels, C. (1978). *The Childbirth Book*. Great Britain: Turnstone Books.

Bieler, L.(Ed) (1963): The Irish Penitentials, *Scriptores Latini Hiberniae*, Vol. V. Dublin.

Blackwell, J (1989). *Women in the Labour Force*. Dublin: Employment Equality Agency.

Bloch, J H. & Bloch, M. (1980). Women and the dialectics of nature in eighteenth-century French thought. In C. MacCormack & M. Strathern (Eds), *Nature, Culture and Gender*. Cambridge: Cambridge University Press.

Blumenfeld-Kosinski, R (1990): *Not of Woman Born, Representations of Caesarean Births in Medieval and Renaissance Culture*. Ithaca: Cornell University Press.

Bourne, G. (1976). *Pregnancy*. London: Pan Books.

Brook, D. (1976). *Naturebirth: Preparing for Natural Birth in an Age of Technology*. Harmondsworth: Penguin.

Browne, T. D. O. (1947). *The Rotunda Hospital 1745-1945*. Edinburgh: F. and S. Livingstone.

Burke, S. (1983). *A Profile of 200 users of Open Door Counselling Services*. Dublin: Open Door.

Callaghan, D. (1970). *Abortion - Law Choice and Morality*. New York: Macmillan.

CARASA (1979). (Committee for Abortion Rights and Against Sterilisation Abuse). *Women Under Attack*. New York.

Chan Shutting H. (1983). Communication to the *writer*. October.

Christiansen, R. (1958): The Migratory Legends, *Folklore Fellows Communications*. No. 175. Helsinki.

Church of England Board for Social Responsibility (1965). *Abortion: An Ethical Discussion*. London: CIO Publishing.

Cullen, L. (1972). *An Economic History of Ireland Since 1660*. London: B. T. Batsford.

Dahlerup, D. (1986). Introduction. In *The New Women's Movement - Feminism and Political Power in Europe and the USA*, D. Dahlerup (Ed). London: Sage Publications.

Daly, M. *Beyond God The Father*. London: The Women's Press.

Daly, M. (1978). *Gyn/Ecology*. Boston: Beacon Press.

De Lee, J. (1920, October). The prophylactic forceps operation. *American Journal of Obstetrics and Gynaecology, 1*.

De Paor, L. The Life of St Brigid by Cogitatus c. 650 (Trans. unpub)

Dean, G. (1984). *Termination of Pregnancy. England 1983. Women from the Republic of Ireland*. Dublin: Medico-Social Research Board.

Donnison, J. (1977). *Midwives and Medical Men*. London: Heinemann.

Dourlen-Rollier, A.M. (1971). In: *Avortement et Contraception*. Editions de l'Institut de Sociologie. Université Libre de Bruxelles.

Dublin Obstetrical Society. (1869 August and November). 'Reports' (Debate on E. Kennedy's paper on zymotic disease). *Dublin Quarterly Journal of Medical Science, XLVIII*, 225-429.

Easlea, B. (1981). *Science and Sexual Oppression: Patriarchy's Confrontation with Women and Nature*. London: Weidenfeld and Nicholson.

Ehrenreich, B. & English, D. (1974). *Witches, Midwives and Nurses: A History of Women Healers*. Old Westbury, NY: Feminist Press/London: Compendium.

Faludi, S. (1991). *Backlash: The Undeclared War against American Women*. New York: Crown Publishers, Inc.

Finnane, M. (1981). *Insanity and the Insane in Post-Famine Ireland*. London: Croom Helm.

Flannery, A. (Ed). (1984). *Vatican Council II: More Conciliar Documents*. Dublin: Dominican Publications.

Foucault, M. (1979). *Discipline and Punish: The Birth of the Prison*. Harmondsworth: Penguin.

Foucault, M. (1980). The confessions of the flesh / The politics of health in the eighteenth century / Truth and power. In C. Gordon (Ed), *Power/Knowledge: Selected Interviews and Other Writings*. Brighton: Harvester Press.

Foucault, M. (1981). *The History of Sexuality Volume One: An Introduction*. Harmondsworth: Penguin.

Freud, S. (1977). *Case Histories I: 'Dora' and Little Hans'*. Harmondsworth: Penguin.

Hannon, P. (1992). *Church, State, Morality and Law*. Dublin: Gill & Macmillan.

Harrison, B. (1983). *Our Right to Choose: Toward a New Ethic of Abortion*. Boston: Beacon Press.

Harrison, B. (1985). *Making the Connections: Essays in Feminist Social Ethics*. Boston: Beacon Press.

Inch, S. (1983). *Birth rights: A Parent's Guide to Modern Childbirth*. London: Hutchinson.

Irish Pregnancy Counselling Services. *Abortion - A Choice for Irishwomen*. Dublin, undated (citing 1980 data from Well Woman Clinic).

Jackson, P. (1986). Women's Movement and Abortion: the Criminalisation of Irish Women. In D. Dahlerup, (Ed), *The New Women's Movement*.

Jackson, P. (1983). 'Women's Reproduction and the Eighth Amendment.' *Bulletin of the Sociological Association of Ireland*. No.35, November.

Jackson, P. (1983). *The Deadly Solution to an Irish Problem Backstreet Abortion*. Pamphlet. Dublin: Women's Right to Choose Campaign.

Jebb, F. (1770). *A Physiological Enquiry into the Process of Labour and an Attempt to Ascertain the Determining Cause of It*. Dublin.

Jennings, J. (1982). Who Controls Childbirth? in *Radical Science Journal*, No.12. London.

Johnston, G. (1870, Feb and May). Clinical report of the Rotunda Lying-in Hospital for the year ending 5 November 1869. *Dublin Quarterly Journal of Medical Science, XLIV*.

Johnston, G. (1871, Feb and May). Clinical report of the Rotunda Lying-in Hospital for the year ending 5 November 1870. *Dublin Quarterly Journal of Medical Science, LI*.

Johnston, G. (1872, Jan and June). Clinical report of the Rotunda Lying-in Hospital for the year ending 5 November 1871. *Dublin Quarterly Journal of Medical Science, LIII*.

Johnston, G. (1873, Jan and June). Clinical report of the Rotunda Lying-in Hospital for the year ending 5 November 1872. *Dublin Quarterly Journal of Medical Science, LV*.

Johnston, G. (1874, Jan and June). Clinical report of the Rotunda Lying-in Hospital for the year ending 5 November 1873. *Dublin Quarterly Journal of Medical Science, LVII.*

Johnston, G. (1875, Jan and June). Clinical report of the Rotunda Lying-in Hospital for the year ending 5 November 1874. *Dublin Quarterly Journal of Medical Science, LIX.*

Johnston, G. (1876, Jan and June). Clinical report of the Rotunda Lying-in Hospital for the year ending 5 November 1875. *Dublin Quarterly Journal of Medical Science, LXI.*

Johnston, G. (1879, Jan and June). Clinical report of 752 cases of forceps delivery in hospital practice. *Dublin Quarterly Journal of Medical Science, LXVIII.*

Jordanova, L J. (1980). Natural facts: A historical perspective on science and sexuality. In C. MacCormack & M. Strathern (Eds), *Nature, Culture and Gender.* Cambridge: Cambridge University Press.

Jordanova, L J. (1984). Women in White Coats, in *The Observer.* London. Jan 22.

Kaufmann, K. (1984). Abortion a Women's Matter; an explanation of who controls abortion and how and why they do it. In R. Arditti, R.D. Klein and S. Minden (Eds) *Test Tube Women.* London: Pandora Press.

Kennedy, E. (1867, Aug and Nov). Important letter from Dr Evory Kennedy to Governors of the Lying-in Hospital. *Dublin Quarterly Journal of Medical Science, XLIV.*

Kennedy, E. (1869, Feb and May). Zymotic diseases as more especially illustrated by puerperal fever. *Dublin Quarterly Journal of Medical Science, XLVIII,* 269-306.

Kitzinger, S. (1979). *Birth at Home.* Oxford: Oxford University Press.

Kitzinger, S. (1985). *Woman's Experience of Sex.* Harmondsworth: Penguin.

Le Guin, U.K. (1989). *Dancing at the Edge of the World.* New York: Grove Press.

L'Espérance, J. (1977). Doctors and Women in Nineteenth-Century Society: Sexuality and Role. In *Health Care and Popular Medicine in Nineteenth Century England,* J. Woodwards and D. Richards (Eds). New York: Holmes and Meier.

MacCurtain, M. & O'Dowd, M. (Eds) (1991). *Women in Early Modern Ireland.* Edinburgh University Press/Dublin: Wolfhound.

McDonagh, S. (Ed). (1992). *The Attorney General v X and Others: Judgement of the High Court and Supreme Court*. Dublin: Incorporated Council of Law Reporting for Ireland.

Macintyre, S. (1977). Childbirth: The Myth of the Golden Age. *World Medicine, 12*(18), 17-22.

MacKinnon, C. (1982). Feminism, Marxism, method and the State: An agenda for theory. In N. Keohane, M. Rosaldo & B. Gelpi (Eds), *Feminist Theory*. Brighton: Harvester Press.

McLaren, A. (1984). *Reproductive Rituals: The Perception of Fertility in England from the Sixteenth to the Nineteenth Century*. London: Methuen.

Maxwell, C. (1956). *Dublin Under the Georges, 1714-1830*. London: Faber and Faber.

Medico-Philosophical Society. (1757). A proposal for furthering the intentions of the society. *Transactions, Medical and Philosophical Memoirs, I*.

Mohr, J. (1978). *Abortion in America: The Origins and Evolution of National Policy, 1800 -1900*. Oxford: Oxford University Press.

Morley, E.J. (1914) *Women Workers in Seven Professions*. London: George Routledge & Sons.

Murphy-Lawless, J. (1988). The silencing of women in childbirth or let's hear it for Bartholomew and the Boys. In *Women's Studies International Forum*, Vol. 11, No. 4.

Murphy-Lawless, J. (1991). Images of 'Poor' Women in the Writing of Irish Men Midwives. In M. MacCurtain and M. O'Dowd (Eds) *Women in Early Modern Ireland*.

Noonan, J. (Ed) (1970). *The Morality of Abortion: Legal and Historical Perspectives*. Boston: Harvard University Press.

Noonan, J. (1979). *A Private Choice: Abortion in America in the Seventies*. New York: Free Press.

O'Connor, A. (1985). Listening to Tradition. In *Personally Speaking: Women's Thoughts on Women's Issues*, L. Steiner-Scott, (Ed), Dublin: Attic Press.

O'Connor, A. (1988). Images of the evil woman in Irish Folklore: a preliminary survey. In *Women's Studies International Forum*, Vol. 11, No. 4.

O'Connor, A. (1991a). Women in Irish Folklore: the testimony regarding Illegitimacy, Abortion and Infanticide. In M. MacCurtain and M. O'Dowd (Eds) *Women in Early Modern Ireland*.

O'Connor, A. (1991b). *Child Murderess and Dead Child Traditions*, Folklore Fellows Communications No. 249, Helsinki.

O'Reilly, E. (1992). *Masterminds of the Right*. Dublin: Attic Press

Oakley, A. (1976). Wisewoman and medicine man: Changes in the management of childbirth. In J. Mitchell & A. Oakley (Eds), *The Rights and Wrongs of Women*. Harmondsworth: Penguin.

Oakley, A. (1980). *Women Confined: Towards a Sociology of Childbirth*. Oxford: Martin Robertson.

Origins, (1984) Vol. 14: No. 21. November 8.

Ould, F. (1742). *A Treatise of Midwifery in Three Parts*. Dublin.

Petchesky, R. Pollack. (1986). *Abortion and Woman's Choice*. London: Verso.

Reid, M. (1990). *The Impact of Community Law on the Irish Constitution*. Dublin: Irish Centre for European Law.

Rich, A. (1977). *Of Woman Born: Motherhood as Experience and Institution*. London: Virago.

Robb, C.(1985). Introduction. In B. Harrison, *Making the Connections*. Boston: Beacon Press.

Rose, R.S. (1976). *An Outline of Fertility Control Focussing on the Element of Abortion in the Republic of Ireland*. PhD Thesis. Insitute of Sociology, University of Stockholm, Sweden

Rotunda Hospital. (1759). *A Copy of His Majesty's Royal Charter for Incorporating the Governors and Guardians of the Hospital for the Relief of the Poor Lying-in Dublin Women*. Dublin.

Rotunda Hospital. (1759). *A Sermon Intended to Have Been Preached at the Publick Opening of the Chapel of the Lying-in Hospital in Great Britain Street*. Dublin.

Saiving, V. (1979). 'The Human Situation: A Feminine View'. In C. Christ & J. Plaskow (Eds). *Womanspirit Rising: A Feminist Reader in Religion*. San Francisco: Harper & Row.

Schrom Dye, N. (1980). 'A History of Childbirth in America'. In *Signs vol. 6 No.1*. Chicago

Shorter, E. (1983). *A History of Women's Bodies*. London: Allen Lane.

Sinclair, E, & Johnston, G. (1858). *Practical Midwifery: Comprising an Account of 13,748 Deliveries which Occurred in the Dublin Lying-in Hospital During the Course of Seven Years Commencing November, 1847*.

Smart, C. (1989). *Feminism and the Power of the Law*. London: Routledge.

Smyth, D. (1992). What is Christian Teaching on Abortion?, *Doctrine and Life*. Vol. 42, May/June.

Stewart, D. & Stewart L. (Eds). (1979). *Compulsory Hospitalization or Freedom of Choice in Childbirth?* Marble Hill: NAPSAC.

Thomson, J. Jarvis. (1986) *Rights Restitution and Risk*. Cambridge: Harvard University Press.

Tucat, D. (1971). 'Les Sages Femmes de Paris à la fin du XIXème Siècle'. In *Penelope* No.5. Université de Paris VII.

Ulster Pregnancy Advisory Service (1984) reported in *Belfast Telegraph*, 7 February.

Versluysen, M. (1981). Lying-in hospitals in eighteenth century London. In H. Roberts (Ed), *Women, Health, and Reproduction*. London: Routledge and Kegan Paul.

Walsh, D. (1975). 'Medical and Social Characteristics of Irish Residents whose Pregnancies were terminated under the 1967 Abortion Actin 1971/72'. *Journal of the Irish Medical Association*, Vol. 68, No.6.

Walsh, D. (1976). *Journal of the Irish Medical Association*, Vol. 69, No.1, Jan 17, pp16-18.

Wertz, D, & Wertz, R. (1977). *Lying-In: A History of Childbirth in America*. New York: Free Press.

Index

For a copy of **Attic Press'**
Women's/Irish Studies List
please write to us at:

Attic Press
4 Upper Mount Street
Dublin 2

Tel: (01) **616128**
Fax: (01) 616176